What is This Thing Called Love?

What is This Thing Called Love? provides a clear how-to guide on the art of psychotherapy with couples from a psychoanalytic perspective. The book draws on both early and contemporary psychoanalytic knowledge, explaining how each theory described is useful in formulating couple dynamics and in working with them. The result is an extremely practical approach, with detailed step-by-step instructions on technique, illuminated throughout by vivid case studies.

The book focuses on several key areas including:

- An initial discussion about theories of love.
- Progression of therapy from beginning to termination.
- Transference and countertransference and their unique manifestations in couples therapy.
- Comparisons between couples therapy and individual therapy.
- Step-by-step instruction on technique.

What is This Thing Called Love? is enlivened with humour and humanness. It is crucial reading for psychoanalytic therapists, psychologists, psychiatrists, couples therapists and students who want to learn about – or augment their skills in – this challenging modality.

Sarah Fels Usher is a psychoanalyst in private practice in Toronto. She is the President of the Toronto Psychoanalytic Society, founding Director of the Fundamentals Psychoanalytic Psychotherapy Program, and a faculty member of the Toronto Institute of Psychoanalysis. Her first book, *Introduction to Psychoanalytic Psychotherapy Technique*, is a psychotherapy guide for students and beginning therapists. Dr Usher is also Book Editor of the *Canadian Journal of Psychoanalysis*.

This book is an important contribution that will help these clinicians develop the skills necessary to work with troubled marriages. Numerous clinical case presentations bring this work to life, clearly illustrating each phase of treatment.

Lewis Aron, Ph.D., Director, New York University Postdoctoral Program in Psychotherapy & Psychoanalysis

The book is filled with rich clinical material and written with great lucidity. Sarah Usher offers to the reader her clinical wisdom distilled after many years of experience, and what is offered is considerable and valuable. The important insights contained in this book will benefit all therapists, including those working with individual patients as well as couples.

Morris Eagle, Professor Emeritus, Derner Institute of Advanced Psychological Studies, Adelphi University

What is This Thing Called Love?

A Guide to Psychoanalytic
Psychotherapy with Couples

Sarah Fels Usher

Routledge
Taylor & Francis Group

LONDON AND NEW YORK

First published 2008 by Routledge
27 Church Road, Hove, East Sussex BN3 2FA

Simultaneously published in the USA and Canada
by Routledge
270 Madison Avenue, New York, NY 10016

Routledge is an imprint of the Taylor & Francis Group, an Informa
business

Typeset in Times by Garfield Morgan, Swansea, West Glamorgan
Printed and bound in Great Britain by TJ International Ltd,
Padstow, Cornwall
Cover design by Sandra Heath
Cover illustration by Graphic Design, Southsea, Hants

This publication has been produced with paper manufactured to
strict environmental standards and with pulp derived from
sustainable forests.

British Library Cataloguing in Publication Data
A catalogue record for this book is available from the British
Library

Library of Congress Cataloging-in-Publication Data
Usher, Sarah Fels.
    What is this thing called love? : a guide to psychoanalytic
psychotherapy with couples / Sarah Fels Usher.
        p. ; cm.
    Includes bibliographical references.
    ISBN 978-0-415-43383-9 (hbk) – ISBN 978-0-415-43384-6 (pbk.)
1. Marital psychotherapy. 2. Psychoanalysis. I. Title.
    [DNLM: 1. Marital Therapy–methods. 2. Couples
Therapy–methods. 3. Psychoanalytic Therapy–methods.
WM 430.5.M3 U85w 2007]
    RC488.5.U82 2007
    616.89'1562–dc22

                                                2007024975

ISBN: 978-0-415-43383-9 (hbk)
ISBN: 978-0-415-43384-6 (pbk)

FOR GARY

Contents

Preface   viii
Acknowledgements   xiv

1 The psychoanalytic perspective   1

2 Getting started: the first three sessions   29

3 Interlude: on love   49

4 The ongoing therapy: technique   72

5 Transference(s)   101

6 Countertransference   116

7 Dénouement: working through and termination   135

   Bibliography   152
   Index   158

Preface

Many psychotherapists and psychoanalysts are aware that a large proportion of their patients spend a significant amount of their time in treatment talking about their experience of intimate relationships. It seems natural, then, that therapists may develop an interest in treating those relationships, *in vivo* as it were, but alas, they may have had no training to do so. It is my hope that this book will provide a guide to experienced, psychoanalytically-oriented individual therapists who want to treat couples, and, as well, will function as a source of supervision for them. I hope those therapists already working in this arena will find the book provides some calm in what can be turbulent waters, as they connect with the stories, feelings, and ideas shared here.

It is somewhat surprising that psychiatry, psychology, and psychoanalysis have not given much attention to treating people in their committed relationships, considering that so much therapy time is spent in analysing the therapeutic dyad. Psychoanalytic theory has evolved significantly over the past half-century: classical Freudian "one-person" theory explored the intrapsychic life of individuals, their drives and defences – drive reduction was the prime motivator; object relations theory focused on our current modes of relating to others, which stem from internal representations of our early attachments – relatedness is the prime motivator; more recently, relational theory moves the emphasis completely to issues of relationship, viewing all psychoanalytic concepts through this lens. (These theories, and others, will be elaborated in the first chapter.) I have omitted several important intervening and contemporary theories here for the sake of making a point: that is, that we are highlighting more and more, in both our theory and practice, the significance of self *in relation* to other. That psychoanalytic theory could be applied to work with couples seems almost self-evident; in fact, a psychodynamic theory of behaviour is especially appropriate for relationship problems. What a simmering stew of unconscious ingredients there is here, bubbling up at times to the surprise of most, if not all, of the participants in this triadic therapeutic interaction. Our early and later concepts apply in spades: transferences, which occur in relation to the therapist, and for the couple, in relation to each other, and countertransference, which can become intense and highly complex. Our old friends, the concepts of resistance and defence, make an interesting appearance here in relation to the therapy as a whole, as well as to the way in which the couple interact with each other. Even *thinking* of the myriad opportunities for projective identification can be overwhelming. As a bonus, because people often consciously and unconsciously see partnership as a means of healing psychic wounds, working with a couple together may provide an opportunity to treat individual symptoms and their aetiology as well as treating the relationship dysharmony. The recognition by the couples psychotherapist of the repetition of unconscious patterns of relating, described in analytic theory, is as important as a detailed knowledge of the facts of the couple's relationship and of each partner's life (Ruszczynski, 1993). Thus, even though at first glance psychoanalysis and marital therapy seem to focus on the observation of different data – psychoanalysis on the intrapsychic, and marital therapy on the interactional – the data observed by both methods overlap considerably (Finkelstein, 1988).

When we see couples in psychotherapy, we find that each partner in the relationship brings a set of conscious and unconscious expectations, and each may feel that in exchange for what they give to the other, they will receive what they want. Sager (1994) refers to these as contracts, and states that each individual is probably operating on a different set of contractual terms, and each may be unaware of the other's conditions. The rules of the game are often changed by one spouse as time goes on, without discussion and usually without the consent of the other. These confusing, often unconscious and vague, disturbances can be made conscious and articulated with the help of a therapist, just as they are in individual therapy. However, as will be discussed later, an interpretation becomes more complicated when three people are participating in it.

The term *expectations* casts a wide net of possible difficulties in couples relationships, from communication, to sex, involvement with in-laws, children, work, and so on. There are many sore spots that can arise as couples proceed through their life together. But these spots have to be quite sore before the couple bring themselves into a treatment they feel may risk undermining the whole relationship.

As this book is being written, the concept of "marriage" has been receiving a great deal of press. Politicians are winning or losing elections because of the way they are defining the term. This controversy about the rights of gay people to marry has brought out hidden, sometimes extreme, opinions on homosexuality, and placed the issue of the "sanctity of marriage" in the arena of political opportunism. This book happens not to contain examples of gay partnerships. Since the psychodynamics of these relationships do not differ markedly from those of heterosexual couples, the therapeutic treatment of these relationships is not essentially different.

I have treated couples for over twenty years and may be one of a relatively small number of psychologists or psychoanalysts who actually received training in this area. In the late 1970s, still the heyday of psychoanalytic thought in Toronto, a psychoanalyst trained in Britain offered lectures on psychodynamic couples therapy as well as instruction on technique. Members of a group of therapists were videotaped over many sessions working with a couple, and these videotapes were reviewed with the rest of the group. Although experience and supervision are necessarily the best teachers,

"Gays and lesbians getting married—haven't they suffered enough?"

this early grounding in the basic tenets of the work has stayed with me in the way I practise, and forms the orientation of this book.

I tend to work long-term with couples, although many therapists use brief treatment models. Analytic experience is the influence here: the more expansive treatment allows the couple to say everything that comes to mind and to learn how to think psychologically about problems before they leave treatment. Once the relationship crisis has subsided, couples are free to discuss topics they did not present with at first – for example, a difficult child who is troubling to them both. As well, longer-term treatment gives people a chance to integrate into their lives together what they are learning and how they are changing. Couples who have busy lives and not enough time to reflect together, and in whom the change in one partner necessarily affects the other, may need considerable time in treatment to effect their mutual adaptation.

I have been focusing above on the complexities, and therefore the difficulties, in treating couples. There is no doubt in my mind that couples therapy is more arduous and draining than individual psychotherapy or psychoanalysis, and also more demanding than group therapy. This may be part of the reason for the sparseness of training programmes and practitioners. I find that I rarely book appointments for two couples back-to-back, as I would with individuals, and I often allow time-and-a-half for a session (previously contracted). The work is at once intense and paradoxically relaxing, as I am more myself with couples, partly because of the speed of the interactions and partly because nothing else works as well. (One countertransference reaction you are practically guaranteed not to have is falling asleep!) There are many intriguing times, touching moments, and a great deal of reward. Couples are often able to express more gratitude for the work accomplished than are individuals.

One aspect of couples work that stands out for me is the contribution of humour to the therapy. In fact, a good sense of humour is even more of a prerequisite for couples therapy than for individual work. Most couples have their own private sense of humour, ways of kidding around with each other – jokes that (re-)emerge the longer the treatment goes on, the more comfortable they feel with the therapist, and the better they start to feel about each other. These lively times, when we can laugh together, are often mutative moments. Using my own sense of humour is sometimes a highly empathic way of tapping in to how one or both are feeling, and can be a way of making an interpretation more palatable: this constitutes an obvious rationalization for the *New Yorker* cartoons, sprinkled throughout the book. Relationships, as we all know, have not only been the subject of songs, plays, movies, and books for all time, but have also been the butt of some very funny jokes.

The contents of this book will draw on the intimate stories of people I have been privileged to know in my clinical work. I have tried hard to disguise them by various means, including using composite descriptions, but they are very real. I am grateful to all of them for the work we have been able to do together and for what they have taught me.

I want to thank Kas Tuters for his inspiration and teaching so many years ago. I very much appreciate that both he and Graham Berman took the time to read the manuscript and offer helpful comments and insights. I also want to thank my husband, Gary McKay, for his continued support, for assisting where he could, and for being able to endure so many lonely weekends during the writing of this book. And I want to thank Mookie, my elderly cat, who curled up on a duvet on the floor of my study all through my writing time, providing me with a quiet and contemplative holding environment.

Acknowledgements

Page 54 – Ten lines from:
"I'm Your Man"
Written by Leonard Cohen
Published by Stranger Music
Administered by Sony/ATV Music Publishing Canada
1670 Bayview Avenue, Suite 408, Toronto, ON., M4G 3C2
All rights reserved. Used by permission.

Page 151 – Excerpt from:
"Little Gidding" in FOUR QUARTETS, copyright 1942 by
T.S. Eliot and renewed 1970 by Esme Valeria Eliot,
reprinted by permission of Harcourt, Inc.

Chapter 1

The psychoanalytic perspective

Couples, married and otherwise, usually come to a psycho-therapist as a next-to-last resort, often after many years of unhappiness. They bring their most private selves, in some way urgently needing to expose problems; in another, embarrassed and shamed by what they often perceive as painful personal failure. Different from patients in individual therapy, they do not enter treatment for personal growth; these troubled people are about to uncover very raw and tender issues with *each other*, and with a third person (referee? judge? parent? friend?) observing, listening, and intervening. It is a tricky and complicated business for all concerned.

Therapists who work with couples are usually inundated with a myriad of dynamics, and so it seems only natural that different attempts to categorize and organize the work have evolved. Although, or maybe because, marital therapy has sometimes been described as a technique without a theory, it has been the object of a great variety of more or less theoretical approaches. Systems theory and cognitive-behavioural theory – including list-making and homework assignments – are popular methods of working with couples. Emotionally focused, brief strategic, structural strategic, solution-focused, narrative, relationship education, and transgenerational therapy are just a few of the chapter headings in the table of contents of the recently published *Clinical Handbook of Couple Therapy* (Gurman and Jacobson, 2002). Contract theory, where both the conscious and unconscious contracts that the couple have made with each other are examined and reworked (Sager, 1994), as well as the search for types or categories of couples that can be put into charts or spreadsheets (e.g. Sharpe, 2000), have also been attempts to cope with the complexity of both the emerging material and the ongoing interactions in the consulting room.

Psychoanalytic theory does not immediately appear to be a natural fit when applied to therapy with couples, since it was developed as a way of observing and interpreting intrapsychic, not interpersonal, data (except transference data, which originally were considered fantasied). Still, it is intricately bound up with the exploration of intimate relationships and, by extension, could be seen as leading to useful methods of treating these relationships. Having a psychoanalytic perspective on couples presenting for treatment gives the therapist the opportunity to bring the concept of the *unconscious* into the work and thus to get an understanding of the unconscious meaning of many of the dysharmonies of the relationship, as well as offering a framework in which to understand the transference and countertransference issues that arise in the treatment – usually not a focus of other types of couples therapies. When a therapist listens to a couple in a psychoanalytic way, they become more attuned to hidden or mixed motivations.

Is the relationship the patient? Or is it each individual? This question of how to formulate the problem reverberates on two levels: theoretically, should we refer to one-person, classical theory in attempting to understand each person who is a part of the relationship problem, or should we refer to object relations, two-person, theories, and focus on the interpersonal quality of their problems? We are not copping out by answering: both. "Emphasis on interaction alone minimizes the complex contribution of an individual's history and psychodynamics, while exclusive emphasis on individual psychology misses the way in which interpersonal interaction governs a couple's intimate life" (Cohen, 1999, p. 144).

Parallel to this, one of the main sources of tension in couples relationships is the need for individuals to grow and develop – to keep *separate* in relationships – and for individuals to connect, attach, and depend – to keep *close* to the other – in other words, the conflicting needs for autonomy and for intimacy. "The management of the inevitable feelings of love and hate towards the same person, which this conflict arouses, is central to understanding the psychodynamics of the marital relationship" (Cleavely, 1993, p. 56).

This chapter will cover the particular concepts from psychoanalytic theory that have, for this author, been most useful in treating couples.

Classical theory

"She said, 'I'll go if you go,' and I said, 'I'll go if you go,' and here we are."

A classically oriented view of couples therapy would, of course, be based on the premise that all functioning is governed by conscious and unconscious phenomena; that an understanding of defences, conflicts, and symptoms is important for an understanding of the individual; and that a person's history explains why specific solutions have been adopted. A clinician applying classical theory to the treatment of intimate relationships would focus on intra-psychic drives and the unconscious reasons for partner choice, listening for evidence of the psychosexual development of each individual, their degree of success in resolving oedipal issues, their pattern of defensive operations, and any manifest compromise formations (symptoms). It is interesting to see how each spouse's conscious and unconscious conflict-ridden or conflict-free motives, that are bound in affect-laden fantasies or mental representations, are played out in the couple relationship, just as we notice how an individual's unconscious conflicts and fantasies are enacted in the therapeutic relationship in analysis or analytically-oriented psychotherapy.

A classical psychoanalytic therapist would make the couple aware that the past is contained in the present and that all thoughts, words, and actions are responses to what has come before. Cohen (1999) summarizes several other psycho-analytic concepts about which one can inform couples during the treatment: overdetermination – that behaviour, thoughts, and attitudes have more than one meaning and can be experienced in more than one way; the idea of primary and secondary gain – that a person might do something for one purpose, while serving another; the repetition compulsion – that we are often irrationally compelled to repeat behaviour that is unconsciously connected to our early experience, both in choosing a mate and within the relationship; and the idea of the observing ego – that it is helpful to step outside of ourselves to see what is going on.

Freud (1914) divided object choice into two types: anaclitic, or literally "leaning on" – the attachment type of object choice; and narcissistic, where the self chooses itself as an erotic object and the person loves what he once was, what he would like to be, or the person who represents a part of his own self. The reader might find the following passage from On narcissism somewhat amusing, although frighteningly relevant:

Women, especially if they grow up with good looks, develop a certain self-contentment which compensates them for the social restrictions that are imposed upon them in their choice of an object . . . . Nor does their need lie in the direction of loving, but of being loved. Such women have the greatest fascination for men . . . . For it seems very evident that another person's narcissism has a great attraction for those who have renounced part of their own narcissism and are in search of object-love. The charm of a child lies to a great extent in his narcissism . . . just as does the charm of certain animals which seem not to concern themselves about us, such as cats . . . .

(Freud, 1914, p. 89)

Narcissistic object choice is evident in the attraction of sameness in the other – which will be discussed throughout the book.

The concepts of transference and countertransference – the unconscious displacement of feelings and attitudes that were intended for someone from the past; resistance; projection; and defence – all of which were born in classical theory, are of the greatest importance in working psychoanalytically with couples. A partner often functions as a transference object, embodying projections and displacements from relationships with parents, and sometimes with siblings. To smoke out these partly unconscious dynamics, the therapist needs a good and thorough history of each individual in the couple, including early memories. History-taking will be discussed in detail in the next chapter.

As well, since classical theory focuses on oedipal time (approximately ages 3 to 6 years) – a period that can sometimes be remembered, albeit in bits – it can help us to understand the triangular relationship with the parents, the desire for and hatred of each parent, and unconscious fantasies about the parents' sexual relationship. During these sensitive years, before the blessed calm of latency, there is an overt re-emergence of sexuality and aggression, usually targeting the parents. As Lyons (1993) says, it is seen as common knowledge that men marry their mothers, even if it is less commonly known that women are sometimes, maybe more often than not, likely to choose mother too. The couples therapist, often a target through the medium of the transferences, can notice how the vestiges of this crucial and intensely conflicted time have hung around in the psyches of adult patients.

Being alerted to the intimate relationship as a place for the re-working of the oedipal conflict, the therapist can comment, if relevant, on the significance in the adult couple of the child's-eye views of parental relationships; of the oedipal issues of inclusion/exclusion; of considerations of gender identity and relationships with opposite-sex individuals; of issues concerning guilt and punishment for presumed bad, or perverted, behaviour; and on the important concept of the triangle, including both being the "third" as a child, and being the couple who excludes the "third."

I find it helpful to assess and understand each partner individually, separate from, and then in conjunction with, the relationship they have created. My own first conceptualization has not to do with drives, but rather with individuals' unconscious motivations and defences, with anxieties and their aetiology. How oedipal issues have been resolved, or not, and how they have affected the choice of partner and the person's capacity for sustained intimacy are of the utmost relevance. Formulating the couple's dynamics will be described in Chapter 2.

In terms of informing technique, classical theory provides us with the tool of interpretation, which proves to be extremely useful in work with couples. Although interpretations usually are not as deep in this modality as they are in individual therapy, interpretative comments can still reflect connections with each individual's past and with unconscious motivation, very helpful in understanding behaviour in the contemporary relationship.

I want to comment here on the capacity to be the couple and exclude the "third," referred to above – in this example, the parents – a perspective that does not get much attention in the literature. Every couple needs a shared private space, from which others are excluded, symbolized by the closed bedroom door. Often that is difficult to accomplish, as we can see from the following.

Carol and Bob, both physicians in their mid-thirties, seen as an ideal couple by their friends, were arguing constantly in private and had stopped having sex for almost one year. Historically, they had dated in medical school and married shortly after. They had two young sons who were cared for by a nanny. As their fights had become more and more bitter, Carol was threatening to leave. They had trouble scheduling their first therapy session because they were both so busy, and Carol could be called to an emergency with very little notice.

When asked about the problems they were having, Carol, a tall, engaging, attractive woman, responded quickly with noticeable pressure of speech. Everything in their lives was a rush. Work was extremely busy, as her hospital was involved in a merger. She was too exhausted for sex, and had to concentrate each evening on organizing for the next day. In addition, her parents, with whom she was very close, lived out of town, and felt they did not see her and the grand-children enough, and certainly not as much as Bob's mother, who lived in town. She worried a lot about this, and kept trying to arrange trips to see them. She usually managed to travel back to her hometown about once a month for family occasions, and her mother sometimes surprised her with a weekend visit to Toronto. Carol also reported that she had a difficult relationship with Bob's mother who, she felt, was extremely critical of her. She stated that Bob never defended her with his mother.

Bob, a heavy-set, determined-looking man, sat sullenly throughout Carol's opening remarks, occasionally glancing around my office as if taking stock of the furniture. His story was briefer: Carol cared more about work and her mother than about him and the children. Her parents, who had a lot of money, and had "loaned" them a large sum when they bought their house, made him feel like he didn't earn enough.

They offered them beautiful paid-for vacations, but the catch was that her parents went with them. Bob's mother, who had been alone since his father deserted the family when Bob was 8 years old, had always depended on him to look after her, as he was the oldest child. He proudly said that he had done a good job of this, tending to her financial and day-to-day needs.

This couple were in therapy for three years. I will extract here one piece of the work for purposes of demonstration. In terms of thinking about them individually, they seemed matched on difficulties in separating from their families of origin (Margaret Mahler's ideas about separation will be discussed in the next section of this chapter), manifested now as a feeling of responsibility for them: Bob felt he had to support his mother financially and when any minor problem arose, and Carol felt that she had to enliven her "lonely" parents with as much exposure as possible to their only grandchildren.

Each could see the folly of the other – i.e. how the other's family interfered with their marriage – and each could be remarkably articulate and insightful about the dynamics at play in the other. Neither could accept that their own concerns about parents were serving the function of keeping them tied to their family of origin, pushing away fears of abandoning or being abandoned by parents, calming fears of being grown-ups in the world, and avoiding intimacy with each other and even with their sons.

In our work together, we talked about their growing-up years. Carol's mother, who needed to know what was going on in her daughter's mind, would climb into her bed with her on weekend mornings and ask her what she was thinking about, how she was feeling, and later, even what was happening sexually with her boyfriends. Her mother was sometimes prone to depression and would take to her own bed for days at a time, absenting herself from the family. As we talked more about this, Carol began to connect these weekend morning talks not only with an expression of loving closeness, but also with the unconscious fantasy of paying this small price to keep her mother from getting depressed. She started to think that seeing her parents so often now may be serving that same function. Her mother's behaviour also had caused her to experience closeness to another as intrusive and self-serving, but something one has to endure to keep people happy. This was part of her intense ambivalence about being intimate with Bob, which she expressed as a fear of being swallowed up by him.

Bob's reaction to this disclosure in our third session was a spontaneous outburst of laughter – partly an expression of relief that this was what had been his wife's worry, and also a reawakening of the sense that Carol was, indeed, a kindred spirit, as he had known all along. "You too!" he said. Bob had been prematurely catapulted into a too-intense relationship with his mother in a different way. When his father left, this was an oedipal victory that was excruciatingly hard to bear. His mother, taking advantage of his natural intelligence and sense of responsibility, blatantly referred to him as her "little man," and asked for his help in caring for his younger sisters, for his advice on which bills to pay, and for his knowledge in how to fix things around the house. She often told him stories about his father, painting him as a mean and violent man, the implication, of course, being that Bob would be different, and would protect her if needed. In our sessions, Bob was much more aware than Carol of his ambivalence toward his mother; he knew he was often quite hostile to her, resenting her demands on him. He said he kept her quiet now by "throwing money at her." This worked for short periods of time. The rest of the time, he and Carol had to institute a telephone schedule with her, limiting the frequency of her calls. (In situations like this, my therapeutic intervention is often to advise getting "call display.")

In this case, both sets of parents constituted the "third," that had to be excluded for the couple to have their own, private space. The guilt and loss that Carol and Bob both felt in contemplating this was palpable. They paid for and took their first holiday with their children and no accompanying others about eight months before we ended treatment. They experienced it with pleasure and freedom. They were able to observe and enjoy their children, who played in the children's camp arranged by the resort, and they were also able to enjoy intimate time together. In our last session, they presented me with a gift: it was a beautiful copper sculpture entitled "The Family." There were two parents and two children standing close to each other. They said that defining their new foursome as their family, and putting boundaries around it, had been the most valuable part of the treatment. We talked about their new fear of repeating this old dynamic with their own children, and they were somewhat reassured that the exposure of it and exploration of the motivations behind it in therapy would help as a preventative measure. They were also able to tolerate more intimacy with each other. The sculpture sits on my filing cabinet.

Work is often a clearly identified "third" for couples in their thirties and early forties. These couples may be in the position of trying to keep their relationship invested, while having very young children who need a lot of attention, and often while one or both of them is at a critical time in their career – as one person put it to me: "If I don't make it now, I never will." This individual, the male partner, whose wife complained that he was not available for her and their 1-year-old daughter, said: "It's interesting. When I'm with the baby, I feel like I'm totally present. When I'm with my wife, I'm thinking about work – and she feels it." He complained that his wife didn't celebrate his successes at work, the rationalization for the significant narcissistic gratification he was gaining being that she would eventually benefit from all this. However, narcissism aside, this is often a legitimately difficult juggling act, for whichever of the partners is working outside the home. It is a pull between two – or three – positives.

Other "thirds" that may impinge can include: the female partner's close girlfriend who likes to have long talks on the telephone, a loved pet, golf, or, for mature couples, older children who keep moving back into the home. When the time and libidinal energy of one or both partners are lavished

"O.K., step away from the laptop and hold up
your end of the conversation."

on someone or something outside the relationship, the
couple's intimacy is usually threatened. Couples may collude
in this if both partners fear intimacy, or if they do not feel
entitled to time alone together.

Object relations theory

This leads us to an examination of the object relations
theorists and their contribution to couples therapy. I will
start with Mahler, as we have just mentioned issues of
separation. In my experience, these issues are often of prime
importance in work with couples.

Margaret Mahler (1963, 1974) refers to

the psychological birth of the individual as the *separation-
individuation process:* the establishment of a sense of
separateness from, and relation to, a world of reality,
particularly with regard to . . . the *primary love object.*
Like any intrapsychic process, this one reverberates
throughout the life cycle. It is never finished; it remains

always active; new phases of the life cycle see new derivatives of the earliest processes still at work.

(1974, p. 3)

Mahler states that in certain toddlers – and we can say in certain adults – the readiness to separate from the mother produces a feeling of panic. In adults, this is often couched as how difficult it will be for the mother, or parents, if the person separates, and indeed, this is sometimes the case. In the couple I am about to describe, Lisa, a 31-year-old architect, was the last "child" left in the city in which her parents lived. Her two (male) siblings had moved to the US, and there was a clear expectation that her role was to take care of the emotional needs of her empty-nested, late-middle-aged parents. However, the panic Mahler describes is complex: for unseparated parents often breed unseparated children. Both Lisa and her mother seemed to feel intense anxiety at the thought of "being out there all alone."

Couples in their twenties and thirties, and even forties, are often encountering quite serious issues of separation from parents, sometimes more evident in one partner than the other. The partnership may have constituted one of many attempts for an individual to leave needy, depressed, sick, angry, or dependent parents. It may seem like a relief at first to establish a new home, sometimes quite far from the parents, but unless the psychological work of separation has been mostly resolved – or at least begun – these attempts often flounder, with the result that the partner takes the hit.

If one partner is motivated, consciously and/or unconsciously, to individuate and the other is not, there will probably be more conflict than if they are more closely matched, unless it is part of their unconscious contract – the reason they need to be together. In most cases, however, the striving partner may describe the relationship as suffocating; the less separated partner may describe it as insecure and fear abandonment.

Once the couple are in therapy, one or both partners can make use of the therapist as both an alternative parent from whom to separate in a more successful manner, and an "adult" giving permission for the separation to occur. For some individuals, often the female partner, there are expressed feelings of guilt and responsibility toward the abandoned parents, sometimes accompanied by separation panic, and this may lead to allowing and even encouraging the parents to impinge in a pathological way on the formation of the new unit. (This is one of the salient developmental hallmarks I always consider during the history-taking when assessing couples presenting for therapy. Have one or both individuals disengaged enough from their families of origin to form a new bond, or is this a source of conflict in the relationship?) One manifestation of the effects of separation difficulties has been described earlier in reference to Carol and Bob.

Colarusso (1990, 2000) refers to the *third individuation*, defined as the continuous process of elaboration of the self and differentiation from objects, which occurs in the developmental phases of early (20 to 40) and middle (40 to 60) adulthood. Colarusso states that Mahler's theories derived from the mother/child dyad are insufficient in and of themselves to explain separation-individuation phenomena in adulthood.

> Adults do not repeat the original . . . process as it occurs in the first three years of life . . . . Issues of closeness and distance must be considered within the context of the primary relationships which shape the *adult* psyche . . . . The major emotional and developmental issues that characterize these relationships (sexuality, generativity, intellectual pursuits, work and play, etc.) are *qualitatively* different . . . and they occur within a physically and sexually mature body and a sophisticated, highly developed psychic structure.
>
> (2000, p. 1469)

Yet, it is still very tempting to see Mahler's stages – particularly her third (rapprochment) and fourth (consolidation of individuality) – as reappearing in the "raw" in the psyches of some couples.

Eric and Lisa, in their early thirties, married with two small children, came to therapy because of Eric's inability to tolerate Lisa's rages, which he could overhear during Lisa's prolonged telephone conversations with her mother; after these conversations, he was usually the object of the "left-over" anger and bad feelings. Lisa's parents had made it clear that they thought Eric – even though he was from the same religious background, socio-economic class, and city – was not a good enough match for Lisa. They found fault with him constantly, and soon were able to justify not welcoming him into their home or summer cottage. In an early therapy session, this couple described how Lisa's mother, during the wedding preparations, had wanted to make an announcement "calling off the marriage." Both partners were able to make it clear that she could call off the fancy wedding, but not the marriage!

In Lisa's intense, screaming fights with her mother after their marriage, she tried to defend herself in every part of her life – job, children, husband, and, of course, frequency of parental visits. Still, her underlying fear of separation from her mother gave her the feeling that she was not defending Eric or herself enough.

Before coming for treatment, this young couple had gone through several periods, often lasting a month or more, where there had been no contact at all with Lisa's parents, because of a presumed insult from Eric to which her mother was reacting to. One of these silences actually occurred during the time their first child was born. There were serious birth problems: the baby was suspected to have a diagnosis of cerebral palsy, and he had to remain in hospital for three weeks postpartum, with either or both parents sleeping over. It was a distressing and very frightening time, but Lisa's parents did not relent. After each prolonged silence, including this one, Lisa capitulated and called her mother; this inevitably led to a repetition of the aforementioned fights.

Eric grew certain that Lisa would become like her mother; in fact, he felt that when he and Lisa fought, she said the same outrageous things her mother said (e.g. swearing, calling him an idiot) and sounded "out of control." He was on the verge of leaving the marriage, as he saw no hope of resolving an issue that he felt was not even his, but that was destroying their marriage.

The thread of Lisa's distressing relationship with her mother was woven throughout our two and a half years of weekly, ninety-minute sessions. It was evident not only in describing direct contact with her mother, but also in almost every fight between her and Eric. Lisa alternated between asking me if her mother's behaviour was "normal," and defending her mother in a way that seemed resistant to change. In doing the actual work with this couple, I found it was best to be straight about how I saw things: to get agreement that we had come upon a knot in the smooth conduct of their marriage, and that we all needed to take the time to focus on it. Lisa's life with her mother was then talked about in depth, with the goal of improving her relationship with her, and with her husband. I offered them an explanation of the process of psychological separation, a learning for both partners. It was news to this couple that the ability to leave parents is a psychological *achievement*, and that it is even possible to form a new relationship with the difficult parent. This idea of rapprochment was beyond both Lisa's and Eric's imagination – especially since they thought that Lisa's mother had to change first.

In this case, my being straightforward with them also served as an attempt to avoid some of the muck and mire of a destructive countertransference reaction of which I was becoming aware: that is, my strong need for Lisa to recognize and acknowledge this disastrous relationship with a mother I had privately diagnosed as a borderline personality; my tendency to side with Eric in his version of the fights; my own rage evoked by stories of this mother's abuse of an intelligent and sensitive young couple; and whatever reflections I had time for about my own issues of separation. (Countertransference responses will be discussed in depth in Chapter 6.)

Lisa's early remembered relationship with her mother was blissful: "She was amazing." They were best friends, and often spent time snuggling on the couch watching TV or reading together. Things changed drastically when she was a teenager; her mother seemed to hate her. "She became opinionated, extremely critical and unbearable – I couldn't do anything right." When we later explored this period in depth, Lisa remembered her father having had a mild heart attack right around this time. She had not previously linked the two events. Her mother's anger at her may have been a displacement from her father, on whom she felt she could no longer depend. Since she didn't feel she could check this out with either parent, we would never know for sure; but what mattered here was that Lisa's perspective on this period of her life (i.e. that she had done something very wrong to incur her mother's wrath) had shifted.

Whenever issues with Lisa's mother were raised in the sessions – and this did not happen every week – Lisa reported she was doing some incredible work, behind the scenes, as it were. She limited the frequency and duration of telephone calls to her mother; she set up a dinner with her father alone; she advised her mother that if she wanted to see the grandchildren, she would have to initiate it. As Lisa had more time to focus on Eric, they found that their sex life began to improve. Then, one week, Lisa announced that she was having serious health problems, and had been to the Emergency Room at the weekend. Her breathing was accelerated and she felt very weak. (A vitamin B deficiency was diagnosed and she began injections!) This episode led to a discussion about her fears of death – which I interpreted as the unconscious fantasy that leaving her mother would cause one or both of them to die. This illness of Lisa's persisted for about one month, as we struggled to work this through. Within about six weeks, Lisa, looking for ways to spend more time with Eric, had come up with the idea of running with him, and almost immediately started to feel great about her body. (Could this have been due to the vitamin B injections?)

The separation from her mother was more and more enabled as Lisa felt more convinced in herself that nothing bad would happen to either of them. She set clear limits for her mother; her mother chose to abide by these limits – most of the time. This process, which also involved Eric and his relationship with Lisa's mother, will be discussed further later.

Much of the psychodynamic or psychoanalytically-oriented writing on couples therapy has been from an object relations point of view. From this perspective, the interactions of the couple would be understood in terms of how each individual's unconscious internal objects are involved and in each partner's perception of and reaction to them. Internal objects may reflect stories, often traumatic, from each partner's early life, and often include the marital relationship of the couple's parents.

In addition to the work of Mahler, the ideas of the British object relations theorists, including Klein, Fairbairn, Bion, and Winnicott, can also be of use in this arena. Even though, as Finkelstein (1988) has pointed out, object relations theories are based on only two observational sources – the psychoanalysis of individual adults and the direct observation of infants and children and their parents – still we can extrapolate from them fairly easily because of the dyadic element. It is worth remarking, though, that it is interesting that observation of adult couples has not played a significant part in the development of theories about object relations.

As has been well documented in contemporary psycho-analytic writing, object relations theorists, beginning with Fairbairn, postulated that libido in infants and adults is not pleasure-seeking, but object-seeking. What we are really looking for is connection with other human beings. Thus the fundamental motivational push is not gratification and tension-reduction, using others as a means towards that end as Freud had postulated in his intrapsychic theory, but con-nections with others as an end in itself. All of the object relations theorists saw the mother–infant and mother–child dyad as of the utmost importance and based their theories on the observation of this bond. The study of how infants and their mothers interact is now recognized as one of the most fertile areas of psychoanalytic thought. That the mother–infant dyad can be seen as the precursor of the husband–wife dyad makes familiarity with this psychoanalytic theory important in work with couples.

As psychoanalytic understanding has deepened and explored yet earlier processes of interaction, so it has aided attempts to deepen understanding of the nature of the couple relationship. The many and complex fears and phantasies, joys and pleasures of earliest object relationships will be reactivated in the interaction between partners, as well as in their joint relationship to the environment they live in . . . .

(Ruszczynski, 1993, p. 20)

Melanie Klein, who worked with very disturbed children, theorized that even young babies struggle with psychotic-like terrors of annihilation and of abandonment. The very deep interpretations offered by Kleinians to their individual patients, both children and adults, are usually not the stuff of couples therapy. However, several ideas from her work are salient. The tendency for children and adults to split objects into loving and hating can often be seen in work with couples. Her theory about the significance of envy can be applied in understanding both the relationship between individual partners, and in the transference – and also in the countertransference, as will be seen later. The concept of projective identification, where one individual projects a bad, or unacceptable, part of the self into another, is an extremely useful way of conceptualizing some couples relationships, as partners are often in the position of mutually receiving each other's unconscious projections. Projective identification is at once a type of defence – keeping a distance from unwanted aspects of the self; a model of communication – putting one's feelings into another person; a primitive form of object relation; and a pathway for psychological change – when those frightening feelings can be re-internalized (Ogden, 1982). Unconscious partner choice, in this theory, is made on the basis of the other's responsiveness to projected aspects of the self – a kind of mutual projective identification society – which Kleinians see as the central mechanism in the establishment of any relationship.

"I'm not quite ready yet. Why don't you come in and make us a drink while I figure out how not to project all my hopes and fears onto you?"

This externalization of the internal conflict into someone who has to be contended with each day may enable that part of the personality to become gradually more tolerable within the self; however, it may alternatively produce a fierce effort to control or punish it in the partner. Tensions within a couple relationship can therefore be thought of as internal conflicts externalized and acted out in the partnership.

(Ruszczynski, 1993, pp. 8–9)

An individual has to find a partner who will contain their projections, and whose projections they are able to contain. In the example of Bob and Carol described above, each person was saying: *You're immature and can't do anything without your parent(s). You're making our lives miserable.* The couple may also attempt to carry out this method of interaction with the therapist, hoping to find an unconscious container for the bad parts of their relationship.

In terms of technique, a Kleinian couples therapist would see the interaction of the two partners as the patient, and would take into account the degree of intensity or force of the projections, how the other partner deals with what has been projected, and how the original partner reclaims the projected contents, if they are able to.

It was Fairbairn, a Scottish analyst who was trained in the British Psychoanalytic Society in the 1930s, who first formulated the idea of object-seeking libido. Fairbairn's theory moved the ego – the whole person – to the forefront of consideration, as existing from birth. He also believed that the ultimate source of psychopathology came from disturbances in the relationship with parents, particularly with the mother, who might fail to provide for the child's dependency needs. Therefore, problems that arise within an adult relationship would be seen as due to a breakdown in the caring component of the relationship, rather than to individual internal conflict. Fairbairn also explained that because the libido is adhesive, the child bonds with the parents through whatever forms of contact the parents provide. If the parents engage in pleasurable exchanges with the child, the child becomes pleasure-seeking. Clinically, Fairbairn was struck by how abused children were intensely attached and loyal to their parents. He noted that as adults, these children will seek painful bonds, since their earlier bonds were painful. This, of course, has significant implications for the choice of a life partner as an adult, and also helps us to understand the fervent hope that many individuals have that their marriage or partnership will heal old wounds, even though they may be burdened with a template of bad object relations. This is a different way of looking at the repetition compulsion, which Fairbairn saw as the need to repeat familiar, even if painful, experiences in order to maintain a connection to the needed object.

Interestingly, while Fairbairn acknowledged the importance of separateness, he stressed even more the need for tolerance

"Wait! Come back! I was just kidding about wanting to be happy."

of regression in adult relationships. In a landmark analytic study of marriage which is still highly relevant, Dicks (1967) emphasized that the tolerance of the needy, dependent, libidinal child is an important part of adult intimacy and attachment. We can see more extreme examples of this in instances when one partner becomes ill, even temporarily, or depressed, and changes the balance by needing to regress and be looked after. In using Fairbairn's ideas, the couples therapist would notice the need of each individual partner for attachment, connectedness, bonding, and caring, and the ability for each to provide this for the other in a flexible, back-and-forth flow.

Different from Mahler, whose theories can be said to stress each partner's capacity for individuation and separation as a major factor in their ability to form a satisfying adult relationship, Fairbairn talked about each person's need for and tolerance of dependence.

Sometimes a split on these dimensions is being maintained by the couple. One partner will constantly express the need for independence, unconsciously knowing that the other will express a need for togetherness. In this type of relationship, if the partner who wanted separateness began to want more intimacy, the other would withdraw. Between them the couple maintain a system that enables them both to avoid what they each fear (Ruszczynski, 1993).

Successful couples somehow manage the "right" amount of each: the ability to be dependent and tolerate dependency needs in the other (Fairbairn), and the capacity to separate from original family members to be able to form new bonds (Mahler) and to be autonomous from each other.

In Bion's model of object relations, the mother's function is to contain those aspects of her infant's experiences, particularly bad experiences, that the infant evokes in her through projective identification. In time, she – the container – is able to process these projections, modify, and make sense of them, and make them available for reintrojection by the infant – the contained. Later, the container/contained becomes an internal structure within the child's own psyche. In an article entitled "Marriage as a psychological container," Colman (1993) explores this concept of Bion's as it applies to work with couples. He points out that an intimate relationship is one of the many arenas that can provide containment for individuals. The capacity to experience it as containing, and to determine the quality of that containment, depends on the degree of the individual's own internal containment, i.e. integration, that has been achieved thus far.

The couples therapist often functions as a container, especially at times when there are complaints of very intense emotions in one partner. For example, one individual may become violently angry verbally and scare the other, who then may withdraw, which usually escalates the first partner's rage. Anne and Michael, both well-known lawyers in their late forties, came to see me because they were fighting so much that they were planning to dissolve their marriage, and their joint professional firm along with it. One of the many issues for both of them was Michael's rage. Anne reported that when he yelled, she and their son would huddle together in fear. Anne presented as a highly rational and reasonable person who, with her obsessional defences, hardly ever made a mistake. This was infuriating for Michael, who saw himself as the "wild" and creative one in the family. Michael, average to small in stature, would often complain that he was seen as a "monster." It took many months of therapy before I actually saw and heard the real thing. Most of the time in situations like this one, the partner who is perceived as having the difficulty won't exhibit it in the sessions as, like everyone else, they are trying to be liked by the therapist, and also they don't feel enough at home. When Michael did get angry in the session, it was not as frightening as I had anticipated (of course, the anger was directed at Anne, not at me!). Once he knew that he could do it, it happened over and over again, sometimes even directed at me.

At times, Michael would be forced to get up and walk out for a few minutes; at other times, he might just pace around the office. I varied my response, trying to understand what he needed in the moment. But most of all, I didn't get scared, and after a few minutes I spoke to him about what had affected him in what we had been discussing. He was able to respond calmly surprisingly quickly, and we went on from there. As this part of the therapy progressed, Anne, fascinated that nothing more happened, and that everyone had survived, sat straighter in her chair and began speaking up. One time, when Michael was extremely angry, I said: "Is this as bad as it gets?" Both chimed in: "Yes!" Now, identifying with me as observer and container, both partners were able to analyse the *interaction* that occurs with this behaviour, and some of the roots for each partner's contribution. This has provided Michael with a modified reintrojectable feeling about his anger, a hated part of himself. Anne, who is no longer scared, is able to react differently whenever it arises, which is far less frequent.

D.W. Winnicott, a paediatrician who became a psycho-analyst, has contributed greatly to object relations theory, and his ideas are particularly relevant to work with couples. Winnicott's writing is so understandable, so human, and so extremely useful (e.g. 1965) that it is not uncommon for analysts in training and experienced analysts to have formed a warm, positive transference to him through reading his work (e.g. Spurling, 2003). The expression "good-enough mother" was conceived by Winnicott to describe the kind of mother an infant needs in order to have an environment to grow and flourish. For Winnicott, the good-enough mother put aside her own subjectivity and focused on that of her baby, adapting herself to the baby's needs and rhythms. Many of his mother–baby concepts are a good fit for couples: for example, we could think in terms of the good-enough partner, who can perform the function of tuning in, at least sometimes, to their partner's needs.

The concept of Winnicott's that seems most relevant to couples work, as it is to all therapeutic endeavour, is his idea of the holding environment, sometimes compared to Bion's concept of containment. Bion's ideas about mothering come from psychoanalysis with adult patients; Winnicott's ideas were formed from his lifelong experiences as a paediatrician, observing real mothers with real infants. Bion tends to see mothers as behaving like a type of analyst; Winnicott sees analysts as needing to behave, at least in part, like a kind of mother – the mother who allows her infant to discover his own inner being in his own way, and in his own time (Colman, 1993). The maternal function here is more of a protective role, an emotionally reliable presence.

To further differentiate between the concepts of containment and holding environment, the example of Anne and Michael is illustrative. In the treatment, I thought of myself as providing containment for Anne and Michael, because I tried to "actively" process the bad stuff (Michael's anger) and make it more palatable and reintrojectable. As well, I try to provide a holding environment for couples, who are surprisingly needy of this and are quick to sense its presence and take advantage of it. This is apparent in the type of material they are more and more comfortable talking about. Anne and Michael had, in the beginning, addressed all their comments in the therapy to me and had needed permission to talk to each other during the session. After one and a half years of therapy, a marvellous event occurred. They turned towards each other and began to work through a very difficult and sensitive issue. They talked for over ten minutes, aware that I was watching – silent – and holding them in safety. Sometimes, while listening, I felt one or the other was missing a point, or that something could have been said more efficiently, but I did not intervene as I knew this fragile experience of their creating a new space for themselves to talk was eventually going to be tried outside of the sessions.

Winnicott's concept of the "third area," that of cultural experience, which he sees as being a derivative of play, can also be explored in the study of the couples relationship. Ruszczynski suggests that this "third area" may be thought of as the relationship created by the couple's interaction with each other.

> The couple relationship exists in the space between the two partners to the relationship . . . . [It] is par excellence the arena for constant interplay between the intrapsychic and the interpersonal. It is pivotal between inner psychic reality (including the perception of the other) and external reality as represented by the otherness of the other.
>
> (1993, p. 23)

A couples therapist becomes increasingly aware of this mutually created arena, as the couple's humour with each other, pet names, and shared history are more and more evident. Also in evidence is the fact that there is so much the therapist does not know about this relationship. This is different from our perspective in individual work, where we have the sense, or perhaps illusion, that we know a great deal about the person we are treating.

Self psychology

Heinz Kohut's (1984) concept of the selfobject and its functions throughout life is a very useful tool in formulating relationship difficulties when working with couples, even though his theory focused on the formation of an individual cohesive self. The most important selfobject function is empathy, the ability to put one's self in another's shoes; the other functions he described are mirroring, twinship, and idealizing. Kohut theorized that when essential selfobject functions are not provided for, individuals may become hostile or depressed. Kohut's stress that we need these functions throughout life, not just as children, was a major contribution to the psychoanalytic literature. He gave adults permission to express the need for another to serve as a selfobject.

In assessing a couple in trouble, we can think in terms of the degree of each partner's ability to provide these selfobject functions for the other, which would make for the achievement of an intimate, satisfying, interdependent relationship. Failure of partners to provide selfobject functions can be a significant cause of feelings of fragmentation, narcissistic rage, and acting out in a relationship (Finkelstein, 1988). We can often determine, during the history-taking (next chapter), what selfobject functions each individual's parents have or have not been able to provide for them and the degree to which they are familiar with the experience, sometimes on both sides, of having selfobject needs met, or of knowing how to do this for others.

Of course, during therapy, the therapist's empathy and the selfobject transferences to the therapist, which become the basis for modelling, are also of extreme importance. When most couples begin therapy, they have lost, at least temporarily, whatever ability they may have had to provide selfobject functions for each other. This was the case with both Lisa and Eric and Anne and Michael. As mentioned earlier, in couples therapy, the therapist–individual relationship is not the only healing relationship in the room. The repair of parental deficiencies in early selfobject functions can play an essential role in therapy with couples, just as it does with individuals. And the motivated couple can learn, by watching the therapist, to provide these functions for each other, thereby affording some healing of past wounds, and learning to be attuned to their partner for the future. In the case of Lisa and Eric, when we were discussing Lisa's failed attempts at rapprochement with her mother, Eric spontaneously said, "I can have a role in this." He saw himself as holding and supporting Lisa, and also as offering new ideas for how to reconnect, even though he himself did not want a relationship with her mother.

Intersubjectivity and relational theory

Intersubjectivity, introduced by Stolorow and his colleagues in 1978, was defined as a field theory or systems theory in which psychological phenomena are understood not as being products of isolated intrapsychic function, but as being at the interface of reciprocally interacting individuals. This view, then, holds that psychopathology in general cannot be considered apart from the context in which it arises and is expressed. Whatever takes place between therapist and patient is determined by mutual influence (Berkowitz, 1999).

The focus on interaction as being the site of the real action is highly relevant in work with couples. The intersubjectivists state that the ability to recognize another person as a separate centre of subjective experience is a developmental achievement, i.e. the acknowledgement of a separate subjectivity with whom to interact. Mutual recognition of the other as separate in work with couples highlights the *me, not-me and then there's you* experience that is lacking in some couples who feel insecure when forced to acknowledge the other's subjectivity.

The concept of the holding environment has been expanded by the intersubjectivists. Ginot (2001) states that the right environment in which an individual can feel understood and held is created by a *combination* of the therapist's empathic listening and the interactive engagement with that individual, which is sometimes stormy and entangled. This engagement leads to increased knowledge about the person's (and to some extent the therapist's) subjectivity and "can offer the patient a profound sense of being understood, and consequently, held" (Ginot, 2001, p. 419). In couples therapy, the therapist's emotional involvement and active participation often places them in the fray of transference-countertransference enactments. This, says Ginot, enhances the holding environment for both people.

Relational theory, which came out of the contemporary American psychoanalytic milieu, is based on Atwood and Stolorow's (1984) work on subjectivity. "The relational-perspectivist approach . . . views the patient–analyst relationship as continually being established and re-established through ongoing mutual influence in which both patient and analyst systematically affect, and are affected by, each other" (Aron, 1996, p. 77). Owen Renik (1993), who invented the rather appealing concept of the therapist's "irreducible subjectivity," emphasized the part the therapist's personality plays in the ongoing mutual dialogue with patients. The couples therapist is always in the mix, and their subjectivity can become the topic of at least limited discussion, considerably more so than in individual work; hence, as I said in the Preface, there is a noticeable lack of sleepy countertransference reactions.

The relational idea that both the transference and the countertransference are co-constructed is very relevant here – but in couples work, the "co" includes three people, instead of two, thereby making for an incredibly rich and productive therapeutic engagement. These issues will be discussed in more detail in the chapters that follow.

To summarize, although I usually formulate a couple's problems using parts of the variety of psychoanalytic theories described in this chapter, my *technique* is a curious mixture; at times, I use classically-oriented interpretation, at other times, I am more completely in the mix in a contemporary/ relational mode. Being free to move in and out, when close attunement to the couple advises, is helpful for the clarification and interpretation of issues, and for role modelling, containment, and safe holding in this complex arena. Each partner can learn to provide a good-enough container, holding environment, and selfobject relationship for the other, just as the therapist provides these functions for the couple.

Chapter 2

Getting started: the first three sessions

"No heroic measures."

To understate it, seeing a couple for the first time is a challenging experience for most therapists. The situation of three separate individuals, sometimes with three different agendas, makes for some remarkable permutations and combinations.

As mentioned in the Preface, there are many ways to work with couples, both in terms of theory and technique. Sometimes conjoint therapy, with two therapists, is the method of choice; or the same therapist will see one partner individually once in a while throughout the treatment as the perceived need arises. I find that one therapist seeing both partners all the time is the least muddy and most efficacious way to proceed. The complications that potentially arise from the two-therapist–two-patient combo are, at the least, confusing. And the practice of seeing one partner individually during couples treatment not only affects the transference (and countertransference), often irreparably, but speaks to a grandiosity that I am not prepared to consciously acknowledge. As well, it takes the action away from the relationship, leads to partner-bashing, or "I've got a secret," and, paradoxically, leaves the therapist in a position of decreased power in the couples session.

My physical set-up consists of my desk chair moved to face the two therapy chairs; the couple sit at an angle, partly facing each other and partly facing me. I start by noticing how a couple have settled in to the waiting room when I go to invite them in: Carol and Bob were involved in a heated discussion about who would attend their son's parent–teacher's night; Lisa and Eric were sitting in silence; Anne was on her Blackberry and Michael was immersed in reading the *New Yorker*.

Presenting problems

Unless they are in extreme emotional crisis, after the first greetings and name and address taking (the therapist cannot assume that the couple have the same last name or live at the same address), I usually begin by saying: "I'm going to ask each one of you why you wanted to come for therapy. It doesn't matter to me who starts, because you're both going to have a turn. So, who would like to begin?"

Hearing that each individual will have a turn limits the "after-you, Alphonse" tendency. Usually one partner says: "Let her/him talk first. She/he's the one who wanted to come." Or: "She/he's the one with all the complaints." Hearing the tip of the iceberg of the relationship problems from each partner's perspective takes the whole first session. I let them know that I will be taking notes during this and the following two sessions. I usually start with a full sixty-minute session; with *some* couples, we move to a mutually agreed ninety minutes.

The odd couple

Mirella and Nick, an Italian couple in their early thirties, were strongly attracted to each other when they met in high school. Because Nick was three years her senior, Mirella's parents would not allow them to date until both were working. They were married when Mirella was 20 and Nick was 23, straight from their parents' homes, and finally were able to have unrestricted sexual activity. Their sex life was always passionate and mutually satisfying; in fact, when they came for therapy after ten years of marriage and two children, they said that their sex life was still great, though infrequent.

In the first session, Mirella said the main reason they were here was that Nick needed anger management. "He puts me down, humiliates me in public with the kids; he yells at the kids and calls them names. He's never hurt me, but he once shoved me. We can't communicate. You can't have a conversation with him." Nick said, "We don't know how to fight with each other. I'm just raising my voice. If I say something she doesn't like, she walks out of the room. I've changed a lot. I can't be myself anymore." They had been to couples therapy twice before for short periods of time and had not found it helpful, except that they were told not to argue in front of the children, which they had tried to avoid. Nick described Mirella as "soft, a push-over, who's teaching our son to be a sissy." Mirella described Nick as "rigid and yelling all the time. He has to have his way." Almost all their fights were about Nick's extreme concern with tidiness in the home, and Mirella's disorganization, hence Nick's referring to them as Oscar and Felix, the odd couple.

It's not me, it's you

Rita and Stan, a couple in their late sixties in a second marriage for both, started their first session with Rita's loud complaints and direct blaming of Stan. "I was divorced for one year, his wife died of cancer. We met three months later. We both wanted to be married again but it's become a horrible relationship. It's his ego – he reacts a lot to any put-downs. Partly because he's a holocaust survivor. He inter-rupts when I'm watching the news. He reads to me when I'm reading. We have problems with money. I have money – he doesn't contribute anything. I've always earned two to three times more than him. Every time we fight, he runs to his kids and tells them. His kids hate me – I said: where's your loyalty. I've lost respect for him . . ." and so on. She described herself as "spewing venom," but always as a justi-fiable reaction to Stan. These complaints went on for more than half of our first session, until I interrupted to invite Stan, who had been sitting quietly and *smiling*, to offer some comments.

Stan defended himself at first: "Rita has said things that are only partly true. I do the cooking and the shopping. I was in a high position in management for ten years"; and then started blaming Rita: "She has a lot of money and she's very tight. She's generous to her children because she feels guilty about the break-up of her marriage. She interrupts when I'm on the phone with my children. One time when she was screaming at me, I thought I was having a heart attack. So I told my son about it." When I asked about his smiling during Rita's opening comments, he said: "I'm not a hostile person. I like things to be happy." On further reflection, he could agree that it might also be a sign of anxiety about being here and anticipating the exposure of their interaction.

For months after this session, this couple seemed to express only anger and hatred to each other. The constant fights and abuse described from home, and which they demonstrated to me in the sessions, made me wonder why they would stay together. These partners could not live together in peace, but were unable to live apart. The triangulation of the adult children into their interaction demonstrated each partner's tendency toward overinvolvement and enmeshment. The blame–defence mode of interacting that was such an integral part of this couple's way of communicating with each other resisted interpretation for a long time, as it served so many functions in their relationship, the most obvious being conflicts around intimacy and abandonment in two lonely, ageing adults who had felt mistreated, unnurtured, and hence untrusting, a lot of their lives. In addition, the persistence of the angry, blaming stance represented a defence against the possibility that one or the other may actually have been able to meet their partner's needs, which had gone unmet for so long, and this may have been felt unconsciously as too painful to bear.

After each partner has had their beginning say, if the other has not already joined in, I ask them to respond to what they've heard. Some of the initial politeness seen in most couples begins to fall away at this point, as they hear either old complaints or new information. A partner may feel embarrassed or angry. Often one individual will cry, sometimes out of hopelessness, sometimes because they have been hurt (again) by the way their partner describes the relationship, sometimes with relief at being listened to by someone who wants to understand.

At this time, usually the therapist can begin to get a sense of the *individual agendas*: not only the reasons for coming, but whether both partners want the relationship to continue, or one is secretly hoping to end it. The amount of anger and bitterness in the room, how long this is sustained, and by whom, is an important indicator. If the complaints appear to be unyielding and are coming from only one partner, if one partner is cold when the other is emotional (crying or angry), if one partner humiliates the other in a sadistic manner about characteristics that are impossible to change, these are indicators that this partner may have already made a decision to end the relationship.

Sometimes it takes quite a few sessions, but often the therapist can tell in the first session that one partner wants out, and this is the motivation for therapy, i.e. they hope the therapist will quickly see how dysfunctional the relationship is and will help to end it, or that one partner will be able to

*"I should ask, before we begin, whether you're looking to
repair your your existing marriage or replace it?"*

tell the other that they want to separate in the therapist's
presence. In this latter scenario, the partner who wants to
leave imagines that the other will be taken care of by the
therapist, so that he or she can get out with less guilt. Some
people come for couples therapy because individual therapy
is too threatening. The motivation for others is to expose a
"sick" partner to a therapist. The hope here is that the
therapist will spot the problematic partner and recommend
individual treatment, thereby confirming who's the sick one,
and also make the sick partner into a better partner.

The *content of the material* in the early sessions is another
gauge of how the work will go. If there have been *in-law or
family problems*, one must consider whether they are such
that one individual has so insulted the other's family, or vice
versa, that one partner has to make a choice between family
and spouse. That choice can be used as a way out of the
relationship. In the case of Lisa and Eric, introduced in the

last chapter, the conflict with Lisa's mother was potenti; fatal to their relationship, and certainly could have been employed as an exit strategy if either partner were planning this. However, although Lisa sometimes defended her mother, she actually agreed with Eric's position, feeling that the worst provocations had been instigated by her mother. Her love for Eric and her fear of losing her parents put Lisa in the middle of a painful tug-of-war. Eric, sensitive to this, did not want to break up their family until he was sure that Lisa could not work this out.

An outside affair, which may or may not be raised in the first session, can affect the therapy throughout, even if there is some indication that it might be "forgiven" enough for the other partner to trust again. Therapists need to ask themselves: does the straying partner really want to terminate the relationship and continue the affair; or do they want to use the therapy to demonstrate why they had the affair – i.e. because their partner is so unappealing, nagging, controlling – and thereby get agreement and redemption from the therapist? Did the other partner come for therapy because they wanted a forum in which to punish the offending partner; or to exhibit themselves as the poor victim?

My experience has been that even though partners may be able to talk openly about revenge, or even to joke about the affair, the memory of this type of transgression fades very slowly in the minds of both partners, if at all – and particularly sticks in the mind of the "victim." Because the partner who had the affair may be heavily invested in denial, and the other partner may be afraid to be seen as bringing up the affair constantly and not "getting over it," the issue may seem to be resolved fairly quickly. The therapist who refuses to collude with this will have to raise the subject themselves at those times when it feels like it is almost in the air. This issue often re-surfaces at the end of treatment.

Blended family issues can be therapy-stoppers if one does not understand the unconscious agendas. For example, in the situation where the children "hate" the new partner and defensively idealize the former one, they may insist that their parent make a choice. The parent may believe they must either lose the new marriage or the "old" children, as the often allied offspring may sense that they have gained a foothold here – as well as an effective way of expressing their rage at the break-up of their family – and become extremely persistent in their negative attitude. This, combined with an individual's possible guilt at leaving a former relationship, can make the new relationship untenable. There may be times in working with these couples when an adjunct family therapist would be helpful.

Serious *cultural, religious, or even economic background differences* can become negative influences as the result of different opinions about child-rearing, or one person eventually feeling deprived of their early family life, where they felt more comfortable. Sometimes individuals are deliberately attracted to a person of a different background from that in which they grew up. This can be exciting for a while, but if it doesn't last, then partners may miss, for example, their former financial freedom, or religious or traditional family activities.

If it seems that there is a significant discrepancy in agendas for coming to therapy, or if the content seems unworkable, the therapist has to explore this with the couple as soon as it becomes clear. In the words of the cartoon that opens this chapter, "heroic measures" might not be in order.

It is at the end of the first session that I explain my approach in working with couples: that the three of us will work together to understand what has brought them to this point; that they will be able to talk about anything they think is important; and that we will take our time with the work, making sure they feel the issues have been dealt with and that ways of working on future problems have been incorporated into their relationship. This last point is stated for the purpose of reassuring them that we will not end the therapy just because the crises are over. I inform them that I will ask about their families of origin in the next two sessions so that I can begin to get caught up with them, to know them better.

I always remind the couple that the fit with the therapist is important, so that they can say whatever needs to be said. Because there are two of them, and they have not had a chance to discuss the session without me present, they are welcome to do this and then call for an appointment in a few days. They also have the option of setting up another meeting right then, with the ability to cancel it twenty-four hours in advance. Although couples rarely leave without making another appointment, I feel it is important to offer them the chance to do so; this demonstrates respect for their partnership and also informs them that I expect them to talk to each other about the session.

History-taking

Unless there is a crisis, I take a complete history of each individual's family life in the second and third sessions, focusing on their early and present relationship with each parent, as well as their view of their parents' marriage.

Their relationship with siblings, which sometimes gains expression in partner choice (more will be said about this in the following chapter), and which is usually clearly enacted in the transference, is interesting and important to hear about. As one contemporary writer put it,

> From the time they are born, our brothers and sisters are our collaborators and co-conspirators, our role models and cautionary tales. They are our scolds, protectors, goads, tormentors, playmates, counsellors, sources of envy, objects of pride. They teach us how to resolve conflicts and how not to; how to conduct friendships and when to walk away from them. Sisters teach brothers about the mysteries of girls; brothers teach sisters about the puzzle of boys. Our spouses arrive comparatively late in our lives; our parents eventually leave us. Our siblings may be the only people we'll ever know who truly qualify as partners for life.
>
> (Kluger, 2006, pp. 31–32)

Sibling issues are particularly noticeable in the history-taking when people report either a complete lack of contact, or extremely close contact, with a sibling. It is often productive to ask: why? Remnants of relationships with siblings can arise in the way partners fight, particularly about sharing household tasks, and in the ways that they are able to play and compete with each other. It is interesting to note whether the partners' experiences in this area match.

During the history-taking, I also ask about their early romantic relationships. This could, of course, be a sensitive area, but I have found that most couples already know this information about each other. I enquire, gently, about first sexual experiences and also about significant long-term relationships and how and why they ended. Of course I never push someone to talk about a past relationship they may not want to discuss. Individuals know how their partners will react to this information better than I do, and I take my lead from them.

"I won't lie. There have been other pussycats."

Individual family histories are loaded with rich material about transference as it will apply to the relationship with the therapist and, of course, as it applies to their partnership. The couple's transferences to each other, their expectations of the relationship, and their attempts to replicate, or rebel against, their parents' marriage and their relationship with their siblings, if applicable, all begin to emerge as one listens to the history. Hearing the description of each individual's early psychological environment helps everyone understand the person's capacity to perform functions of attunement, containing, and holding for their partner, and to communicate their emotions and needs to the other.

The process of taking one partner's history in the presence of the other is extremely productive. The therapist can observe whether each can allow the other to have the complete spotlight and to talk without correcting them (e.g. "No, you're wrong. Your mother is actually very controlling!"). We can observe whether they are listening with interest, whether they seem bored, angry, anxious, or even sad.

I have had several experiences of one partner crying during the other's story. Anne became very sad when Michael talked about his brother who had moved away. She told us that they had been very close to him and that she really missed him now – this was news for Michael. In the case of Chantal and Brad, both engineers, to whom the reader has not yet been introduced, Chantal was emerging from the break-up of a torrid affair with a colleague, and was certain she wanted her marriage to Brad to end. She had only complaints and negative comments to make about Brad, partly by comparison to her idealized lover and partly as justification for the affair. Yet, when I was taking Brad's family history which, because of the crisis they came in with, only happened several weeks into the treatment, Chantal warmed up for the first time, laughing hard about the foibles of his parents; she joined in with other stories about them, which they both shared in a surprisingly warm and humorous manner. This gave the process of history-taking an added usefulness in the therapy, as it actually provided for a shift in Chantal's (defensive) critical attitude and, as a result, in Brad's self-protective defensiveness. I use the term "surprisingly" to highlight again that, as couples therapists, we know less than we think we know about the couple we are treating. They have lived a history together; we are the outsiders here.

If they haven't already done so, I ask each partner to react to what they have heard – whether there was anything new or surprising in the information, and whether they would like to give their version of the partner's family. This provides another perspective, which can be very meaningful for the other partner as well as for the therapist. In my experience, partners always know the facts of the other's family history; however, they sometimes have not anticipated how their partner *feels* about what has happened in growing up – in other words, the tone of the affective meat on the factual bones. Interestingly, as couples learn to work together in therapy, they will often remember the affective emphases from the history-taking sessions; this allows them to contribute to their understanding (and interpretation) of the difficulties they are having. This is co-participation at its best.

After the individual histories, I ask about their relationship, including how they met, the climate of the courtship, and any break-ups along the way. I ask what attracted them to each other, which usually presents the first opportunity in the sessions for warm fuzziness, as partners reminisce about the other's strengths, sex appeal, and admired personality features. During this time, we may all note how these feelings have been lost or changed, and sometimes we notice how the very qualities that attracted in the beginning have become irritants. Sometimes we just enjoy the view.

Critical incidents

In taking the history of the relationship, I watch for what I call *critical incidents*. These are occurrences, usually in the joint past of the couple, that had the effect of changing the course of the relationship, and may or may not be known to the couple. Sometimes the incident seems blatantly obvious: Chantal's affair, for example, was an obvious critical incident. Could their marriage survive this? Sometimes critical incidents are buried in a number of other crises that did not have the same near-fatal effect; sometimes the incident may have occurred so far in the past that even the therapist does not recognize it as a critical incident. In taking Chantal and Brad's marital history, I was able to detect a number of other incidents in their past together which may have contributed to this latest critical incident, so, let's meet Chantal and Brad.

This couple had both completed masters degrees at a graduate school in Vancouver. Then Chantal had gone on for her Ph.D. to become an academic, while Brad had secured a high-powered job in their common industry. Chantal was soon offered an exciting teaching position in Boston, and although Brad loved his job in Canada, he agreed to go. The new job he found in Boston involved Brad in a fair amount of travel and Chantal was left on her own with their new baby a lot of the time. She became depressed for the first time in her life. They decided to have a second child, and this led to further isolation for Chantal, both from Brad, who was travelling, and from her professional life. In telling the story, neither one was aware of Chantal's having been depressed until I labelled it, and certainly neither was aware of the anger she had stored up against Brad for not being there, nor of the anger he had stored up against her for the move. During this early stage, I highlight what I have heard, either by repeating it with emphasis, or by checking with the other partner as to whether they would agree with their partner's account. I may or may not offer an interpretation at this point, depending on the receptivity of the two individuals.

The empty nesters

When Diane, part of a middle-aged couple, called to make an appointment for herself and her husband Tom, she was crying. "We've been married for thirty years, and our kids are all grown up. This should be the happiest time of our lives together, but it's been terrible. I don't know what's wrong."

In their first session, this couple appeared to be cautious in what they reported to me, protecting each other and the marriage. Tom, a driven and successful businessman, had seemed unwilling to come; Diane, a housewife who was starting a small business in their home, was desperate. The critical incident that motivated her to call was their youngest

"Well, now that the kids have grown up and left I guess I'll be shoving along, too."

child's leaving home. They described a family life that included much travel together and many elegant dinner parties for "Tommy's" clients and business associates, catered by Diane, but I did not hear of any intimate time between them that was fun or enjoyable. Tom's social and emotional involvement seemed to be at the office and the gym. (He proudly told me he could beat a 30-year-old at squash.) The now absent children seemed to have been the recipients of the displaced love they were unable to give to each other; they described the children as being "a huge focus of energy and attention." After the history-taking sessions, Tom called me to ask for an individual appointment. Suspecting it was "I've-got-a-secret," I said "No, we have to keep it in the threesome." I later went back and forth in regretting this decision, as I started to think that maybe I could have helped him, without bringing Diane into it.

In the next session, I heard about the most marvellous critical incident. Diane had served as a surrogate mother for her sister's baby, since her sister had uterine cancer. This was fifteen years ago, but had put an enormous strain on the marriage and on the family unit. She had been artificially inseminated with her brother-in-law's sperm. A highly complicating stressor was that they decided to keep the whole pregnancy a secret, as it was illegal, and Tom was worried about trusting their neighbours and friends. Tom was present at the delivery, trying to be a supportive husband, but in truth things were never the same between them again. In addition, Diane felt a bond to the child (a boy), and couldn't spend enough time with him and her sister (who had survived the cancer), which also put a strain on her relationship with Tom and their two daughters. I could only imagine how guilty Tom must feel if he, indeed, were being unfaithful to this angelic person. I must have communicated something, because somehow whatever was distracting him seemed to get resolved after two months of our sessions, and Diane reported he was much easier to live with. We then explored, in detail, the time of this pregnancy and the aftermath. Again, this couple did not present with this problem – maybe they were still trying to keep it secret – and only mentioned it in passing when we were talking about these years in their marriage. They had colluded to not identify it in treatment as a turning point for them – it was too charged.

In another instance, I saw a couple who had endured an abortion, approximately two years before coming for therapy. Neither one even mentioned the abortion until much later in the treatment. The female partner, as it turned out, had never forgiven herself or her spouse for this event, but felt it was not appropriate for her to talk to him, or anyone else, about it any more. In the case of another couple, the wife had supported the husband through many years of study, which had been agreed upon by both, and had built up a great deal of anger and resentment about this. They came for treatment well after the period of study was finished, when the husband was employed in his chosen field. The wife did not know why she was so angry; she was only conscious of wanting to separate.

Other critical incidents may involve one partner's prolonged illness or the loss of a job; in these situations, the
other partner's anger may be regarded as an unacceptable
and selfish response, and so it is hardly conscious. Sometimes
the death of a parent can constitute a critical incident, not
only in its obvious effect, but more insidiously in how the
other partner responded – were they helpful or distant, were
they able to hold the grieving partner in the way that was
needed. Seemingly smaller occurrences, such as a parental
visit where one partner feels betrayed, or one partner's negative response to a vacation that went bad, or even something
particularly hurtful that was said during an argument, can
become a critical incident, that is, a turning-point in the
relationship. There is more chance of built-up anger, resentment, or hurt becoming a fatal critical incident when the
other partner is not aware of how their partner is feeling,
which happens surprisingly often. "She was building a file
on me and I didn't even know it," one man said to me. Are
women more guilty of either harbouring negative feelings
and/or not communicating them?

"If you ask me what's wrong one more time, I'm going to tell you."

Often having a baby constitutes a critical incident as a couple's together life is, at least temporarily, affected; their attention is focused on the baby and not on each other (this may be more true for the mother); their time together is extremely limited; and they are trying to function with considerably less sleep. Everyone recognizes this, yet sometimes the changes after the baby are subtle and go consciously unnoticed. New mothers are often not interested in sex, and their partners are forced into the nice guy position of trying to be sensitive, while not getting much else in the way of affection and attention. Sometimes women do not resume their former sexual interest for a year or more, which may permanently affect the tone and quality of the couple's sex life. This happens in an underground way, and is usually not raised spontaneously by the couple as a presenting problem: the wife may not have realized it; the husband may feel it is boorish to raise it.

Although some of the time these incidents may have been felt as a nagging irritant, they may not have been seen as critical by the couple until highlighted and explored by the therapist. The partners need encouragement to see these incidents as critical, and to talk to each other about them, sometimes for prolonged periods of time. There are times, of course, when partners cannot forgive, when one incident or several incidents have become too ingrown in the relationship, and when the damage that has been done is so great, that the relationship may not be able to be saved.

Critical incidents may become apparent during the first session when discussing the presenting problems, or while taking a history of the relationship. However, the couples therapist still has to be alert for their appearance later on in the treatment.

Sex as a critical incident

The now familiar question: "Is there sex after marriage?" has ceased to be surprising or even funny. As we know from our work with individuals, an active sex life in committed couples

"Don't get your hopes up, Buster."

cannot be taken for granted. Often couples will spontaneously volunteer information about their sex life in the first few sessions of the therapy as they are explaining the problems in their relationship. If, however, they do not, then it is wise to ask, not only to get the information and to educate couples that this is something we can talk about here, but for other reasons as well. There may be an embarrassing problem which one partner believes they are protecting the other from by not discussing (e.g. impotency, a lack of hygiene). There may be practices that one partner is unhappy with which they feel cannot be discussed. For example, in one couple I saw, the woman, an ardent and well-known feminist, had submitted to being tied up by her male partner during sex against her own wishes. She did not enjoy this, but felt her partner would leave her if she didn't cooperate. Often significant differences in level of desire make individuals reticent to speak. Many couples have more difficulty communicating with each other about sex than about any other part of their relationship. This makes it all the more necessary for them to know that they can use the holding environment of the therapy to talk in detail about these very private and sensitive issues.

Having said this, however, I do not usually make a couple's sexual life the focus of our work together, even if they start with this as the presenting problem. My view, like most of the psychoanalytic theorists described in the last chapter, is that sexual problems are an integral part of the relationship: sexual activity usually expresses needs for love, desire and being desired, caring, dependency, attachment, holding, and intimacy. Sexual difficulties are often indicators of difficulties in these areas of the relationship.

Formulation

In starting therapy with individuals, it is extremely helpful to think through a beginning *formulation* after the history-taking. With couples, I tend to do three, very tentative, formulations. After each person's history, I write a brief formulation of my impression of that individual, a sense of their personality or character, each individual's object relations, the defence mechanisms they tend to employ, and a hunch about how they may be contributing to the relationship difficulties. I note particularly their relationship to each parent and their view of their parents' marriage. The third formulation is about the relationship, which usually comprises a brief paragraph on the relationship as patient – critical incidents, hurdles that have been too big to jump, sensitive areas, any areas of collusion between the two, and the natural strengths that have evolved over their time together. As well, I attempt to identify the more unconscious forces that flow between the partners, indicating bonds of a positive (loving) or negative (hating) kind. This latter aspect constitutes the psychological core of the couple's life together, not only in the disorders of the relationship, but also in the healthy, normal functioning process that binds two people into a pair: a whole that is greater than the mere sum of its parts (Dicks, 1967).

All of these thoughts about a formulation are necessarily very rough, as I keep in mind that there is an entity here of which I am not a part, and for which I have great respect. But

I do find it helpful to write something, and I also find it helpful to keep fairly detailed notes after each session as the work progresses. There is a lot to remember – in the names and personalities of the family, friends, colleagues, and fantasies and dreams – of the two individuals.

Chapter 3

Interlude: on love

> Here goes, Baby
> Here goes
> Every worry, every fear goes
> Every dull day in the year goes
> I'm about to fall in love . . .
> (Frank Sinatra, "Ratpack") (composer unknown)

Falling in love

As psychotherapists and psychoanalysts we do not have an exact definition of love; still, we are all certain that we know what the term means – it is just hard to articulate.

> "Sexuality," "romance," "love:" words that should be easy for the psychoanalyst, for they refer to direct, reportable experiences with visible behavioural consequences. Words that draw on common knowledge requiring at the start neither the microscope of analytic treatment nor the dark glass of metapsychology. But these words are not easy to encompass.
> (Stoller, 1991, p. 413)

We know the feeling of longing; the fortunate among us know the ecstatic joy of being submerged in love; and most of us know the aching experience of the lack of it. We know this bittersweetness through our deepest selves, and we know it vicariously through the love affairs of our patients and our friends. Almost every book we read and film we see is based on love; in fact, nothing is interesting without it. Most of us, sophisticated as we are about life and even about analysis, would subscribe to the Beatles' dictum "All you need is love." After all, isn't that what we secretly think "cures" in psychoanalytic therapy? Some of you may be reading this chapter right now in the hope of learning something new about this mysterious and elusive state. I hope you will not be disappointed.

"Falling in love is the nearest most of us come to glimpsing utopia in our lifetimes" (Kipnis, 2003). When we think about the happy beginning of love, being uncritically adored and adoring, it seems like an altered state. Are we in our right minds? Shakespeare wrote: "Love is merely a madness." The extreme highs and lows are reminiscent of a bipolar disorder; the preoccupation with our lover could very well be an obsessive compulsive disorder; the splitting of that precious object into all good – with others as not measuring up – smacks of a borderline personality disorder; our aching desire to be with the person classifies us as having a pathological need for symbiosis – or at the very least as being co-dependent; and our sudden intense hike in sexual passion feels like a large dose of nymphomania. In fact, changes in brain and blood chemistry of those who claim to be madly in love have been found scientifically to be close to the changes observed in people with severe obsessive compulsive disorder.

From the psychoanalytic vantage point, as from the perspective of certain parts of society, the desire and longing for another person inevitably threaten the status quo, the institutions that regulate and contain people. Thus, the emotions of love threaten the rule of the mind, and may be disturbing to psychoanalysts, as they have been to so many philosophers (Ross, 1991).

Stoller states that what differentiates the concept of love in all its iterations from the concept of romance, or *being in love*, is minimal fetishizing. Which implies, in varying amounts, empathy; identification; the need to need and the need to be needed; high-pleasure altruism; reduced inventing the other to fit our primordial fantasies; not too much ego ideal or other idealizations; the capacity to survive one's own and the other's rage and fear (stoically, with good spirits, even with humor); curiosity; . . . respect: admiring and unmalicious envy; capacity to keep one's boundaries in the midst of merging; . . . happy vulnerability.

(1991, p. 414)

This sounds like a perfect recipe: a soupçon of this, a dollop of that; if only one could manage and measure out the ingredients, one could produce a perfectly delicious stew. The capacity to retain one's senses and one's reason while one is being joyously swept away in idealizing and merging with another is sometimes too much to ask, even from an experienced chef.

Idealization

"Idealization is the mental process by means of which the object's qualities and values are elevated to the point of perfection" (Laplanche and Pontalis, 1973, p. 202). Most analytic writers (e.g. Garza-Guerrero, 2000) have understood a lover's idealization as the projection of the ego-ideal onto the object of their love, a seeking to re-encounter a paradisiac state of lost childhood narcissism. With this interpenetration of self and other in passionate love, falling in love seems to make for an expansion, rather than a depletion – as was earlier hypothesized – of the sense of self, and for an awareness of the complex nature of the beloved (Ross, 1991) – albeit as seen through the rosiest of glasses.

Certainly, at the start, every good characteristic of our lover is heightened. This individual becomes the most desirable person in the world, embodying the powers of understanding of Winnicott, the sexual preoccupation of Freud, and the capacity for empathy of Kohut. As we have seen, initial idealizations reflect not only the warm glow of past loved and idealized objects, but also our hopes and dreams for the future, projected onto this one person. Negatives or flaws that may slip out in the idealized one can often be recognized intellectually, but they are usually either disregarded, or rationalized as endearingly special. In our state of idealization, if we don't readily see all the personal characteristics we require for loving someone, we just *assume* that our chosen lover possesses all of them. Idealizing is another of those key processes that distinguishes falling and being in love from loving (Sharpe, 2000).

Some of us are better idealizers than others, primed for the fulfilment of the wish for the perfect partner who will make us feel wonderful about ourselves and about being alive; a lover who will complete us – be our "better half," be the longed-for minutely attuned selfobject, who will compensate for perceived deficiencies in our own selves, and who will be an external match for the love relationship we have already created in our minds, based on loving and being loved by important people in our lives, or the lack thereof. Others have trouble idealizing, sometimes due to the premature discovery of some unlucky object's feet of clay, and these individuals remain cynical as a defence against the pain from the inevitable disappointments in love; they have more difficulty falling in love. As Fairbairn and the object relations theorists have stated, our way of connecting with new objects will be based on the quality of connection we had with our early objects. Being loved for some people may mean being nurtured, for others being revered, for some being devalued, or even abused.

Merging

As has been mentioned, the process of falling in love also includes the sense of merging with the idealized person, a blurring of boundaries between self and partner. In a way, we *want* to lose our limits – despite Stoller, cited above – to understand completely another person, to live for them more

"I'll be right back—I'm going to blink."

than for ourselves. Bak (1973) comments that the state of being in love aims towards the fusion of self and non-self, and undoubtedly, too, the imagined blissful fusion of the infant with the mother. The almost obsessive preoccupation of the lover with the face of the beloved may well be a regression to the beginning of object formation: the recognition of the mother's face. Lovers gaze adoringly into each other's eyes, engage in a lot of physical touching, and want to be together all the time.

Sex and passion

We hope to at least begin our love relationship with wild passion. Passion, it turns out, involves more than sex and orgasm. Passion involves a yearning to be with the loved one – which implies there has been a separation – and it is passion that is infused with ambivalence. Consider these lyrics from one of Leonard Cohen's songs of desire:

> If you want a lover
> I'll do anything you ask me to
> If you want another kind of love
> I'll wear a mask for you
> If you want a partner
> Take my hand, or
> If you want to strike me
> Down in anger
> Here I stand
> I'm your man.

(Leonard Cohen, "I'm your man")

He speaks of passion as a mixture of sacrifice and potential pain. This powerful mixture combination in Cohen's lyrics is inherent in all passion, which encompasses erotic excitement, aggression, hurt, and tender feelings. As Freud said throughout his writings, hate, the opposite to love, is its constant companion, therefore ambivalence, the co-existence of love and hate for the same person, is the most natural and most common of conditions. For the lovers, sexual excitement has to incorporate aggression in the service of love (Kernberg, 1991).

Lina Wertmuller's 1974 film, *Swept Away*, in which an upper-class Italian woman and the yacht-hand aboard her ship are stranded on a deserted island, is a moving and disturbing (and unsublimated) example of this. Mariangela Melato is the classic "rich bitch." She defends against her anxiety at being lost at sea with someone of the lower classes by coming on strong – alternatively striking provocative poses in her revealing clothes and sounding off about politics and other topics. Her loud and grating voice dominates the first half of the film. Giancarlo Gianni seems to be quietly enduring this display, with only minor eye-rolling, while struggling for their survival. He retains his role of the servant until they reach the island. The film then turns on his rage and aggression, which are finally expressed in his denying her food and shelter, in excruciating humiliation, and in disturbing physical violence. It all leads to such fiery passion that the audience itself is swept away. There are very few tender moments in this film; yet we marvel at the obvious poignancy of their love for each other.

It is difficult for psychoanalysts to conceptualize what is sexy about sex. All this talk about libidinal impulses and achieving genital primacy just doesn't cut it somehow. Ross (1991) tells us that whatever happened to Sigmund Freud's relationship with Martha, his voluminous letters to her as his fiancée are among the most moving examples of passionate feeling "in the Western world." Somehow, his theories, and those of his followers, were unable to capture these emotions.

Stoller (1991) throws into the mix that there is often erotic incompatibility between men and women, and an incompatibility, in males more than females, between erotic excitement and love. He cites research on "pornography" that shows that most women prefer scripts that include tenderness, intimacy, and caring, whereas men may prefer fetishes, or dehumanized objects. "A woman's aphrodisiac is a man's soporific," he states.

But somehow, heterosexual lovers do manage to experience great pleasure together, and homosexual lovers find enough differences to trigger intense passion.

Object choice

Freud's (1910, 1912) hypothesis about *object choice* was that it should be understood as the re-finding of an old object. This idea is still prevalent, in different iterations, in contemporary analytic theory. The struggle for the individual of needing an object that is reminiscent of a past idealized love, i.e. mother, but at the same time of needing to avoid or keep under repression incestuous wishes, is one which Freud said neurotics often cannot manage. Every new love contains a triumphant overcoming of the incest barrier.

"I married Norman when minimalism was all the rage."

There is a German expression, "For every pot, there is a top." Sometimes it is hard for us to understand a person's object choice, especially when we are not familiar with their background; sometimes the triumph over the incest barrier seems pretty thin. Why did the relationship between John Lennon and Yoko Oko shake the world the way it did? OK, so it broke up the best band there ever was – but there was an eeriness to it that was hard to name. Yoko was older, her face was hidden by her long, black hair, and she hardly ever spoke (the perfect projection screen). Yet, it was remarkable how John needed her. She enabled him, he thought, to be his real self (the perfect mirroring selfobject). What power did she have over him? In reading about John's early life

(Lennon, 2005), one is impressed with the absence of both of his parents – his father, a seaman, was away all the time, and then left his mother when John was 4 years of age; his mother, who had an affair when John was 5, got pregnant again and, as a result, was forced to give John up to the care of an aunt during this turbulent (oedipal) time. Did Yoko represent his memory of his mother, from the age of 0 to 5 years? Was she the wished-for idealized mother he never had – totally focused on him? Did she represent the ultimate oedipal victory over all his mother's lovers? Or was she the absent father, recaptured; or the strict aunt, triumphed over, and now giving permission for him to do as he pleased?

In *On the universal tendency to debasement in the sphere of love*, Freud (1912) discusses the Madonna/whore resolution to the difficulty of triumphing over incest: in his words, men seek as sexual objects women they do not need to love in order to keep their sensuality away from the ones they can love. Debasement, therefore, is a defensive manoeuvre to protect against the object being too closely associated with the prohibited incestuous object which must remain pure, unlinked with sensual desire, and thus overvalued.

It is interesting to think about Freud's theory as one of the possible components in the psyches of partners who have affairs after marriage, sealing off sexual excitement from their committed relationship. (Is this what Freud was up to – in a highly sublimated form, of course – with his sister-in-law Minna?) Often people who masturbate with pornographic magazines or the internet will be conscious of keeping this "sleazy" (to quote one of my patients) part of themselves separate from their spouses.

Romantic, passionate love seems to manifest itself in much the same way in all age groups – most closely resembling the flowering of love in late adolescence. Many older patients, even elderly ones, who fall in love, whether for the first time or not, talk about waiting for telephone calls, the first hand-holding, and the first kiss – all blushingly described. It is as if they are embarrassed by the intensity of these steps in the process, believing that when one is older, one should not be "necking," but should proceed, without much ado, to perfectly compatible consummation. This is not the case – which is why everyone can relate to love songs, movies, and stories.

Often it is clear in treatment that conflictual early relationships are recaptured and restored through complex re-enactments in marriages. In these situations, individuals repeat familiar, painful aspects of the early relationship and rework them in an attempt to master them. It sometimes appears that the couple in treatment have consciously, manifestly chosen the exact opposite of past objects, perhaps in an effort to override unconscious incestuous wishes. It is these superficial differences that attract; for example, what Bob loved about Carol was her tall, gangly body, her dark hair, and her sweet face. His mother and sisters were stocky and blonde, quite different looking from Carol. Yet, as they grew to know each other better, he found that he perceived Carol, like his mother, to be demanding more from him than he could give. Because this "similarity" unconsciously became an interference with their previously passionate sexual relationship, we focused in therapy on the *differences* between Carol and his mother to jump-start things between them. Brad, from a western WASP family, loved the fact that Chantal was French Canadian – her voice, her dress, her closeness to her family were all characteristics he associated with this difference in cultures. We could hypothesize, in fact, that the prevalence of interracial and inter-religious marriages in our society represents a strained attempt to bypass incestuous wishes.

In addition to oedipal issues, the role of siblings mentioned earlier, in an individual's life can also play a part in their choice of a lover. Growing up with an opposite-sex sibling can launch one into the sexual arena with more comfort and confidence – that is, if the relationship has been untraumatic. This has been referred to in the first chapter. However, sexual and aggressive impulses may be acted on by either-sex (usually older) siblings, which can leave a mark in terms of later relationships.

Sharpe and Rosenblatt (1994) used the term *oedipal sibling triangles* to describe the triangles that develop between siblings and between siblings and a parent which exhibit many of the characteristics of the traditional oedipal triangle. They state that love and hate between siblings can be very intense, as can erotic feelings, whether fantasied or acted on, and that an idealized sibling can have a profound effect on object choice – for example, in one couple they describe, the husband could not compete with an idealized older brother. I have seen a male partner who often enough made the slip of referring to his wife by his younger sister's name; in another couple, the female partner was married to someone like her father, but had a torrid love affair with someone who reminded her of her older brother. Some couples relate as siblings more than others – competing, joking around, teasing each other, and having difficulty with the passionate expression of sexual feelings.

Actual, usually explorative, sexual experiences with a sibling are common enough and are not talked about in the history-taking, but if they have been traumatic, their effect can be inferred from some of the problems that arise. Intense, if fleeting, erotic activity with a same-sex sibling can have an effect on sexual identity in choosing a partner.

Sibling aggression comes up more often. In the case of Lisa and Eric, Lisa reported having been victimized by one of her older brothers. He used to pin her down on the floor and pretend to spit in her face. Sometimes he would torment her with insults. In fact, it was hard for him to pass by her without punching her. Eric's parents had been divorced when he was a teenager because of his father's angry outbursts. Before the divorce, Eric used to pick on his younger brother. In one session, he talked about throwing his brother's blankets and his clothes out the window onto him when he came home from school. Since his parents' divorce, his need to identify with his father had decreased, and he had become quite mild mannered. When he talked about his victimization of his younger brother, Lisa cringed. Here was an example where an aggressor had married a victim, each trying uncon-sciously to tame, or do right by, the other. During the treatment, this broadened the discussion, as Lisa began to

understand more deeply her sensitivity to any sign of irrita-
tion in Eric. As well, her fights with her mother were seen as
an opportunity for her to identify with the aggressor and also
to express her anger at her mother for not having protected
her during those hurtful times.

After one has found one's lover in spite of, or because of,
the above, how do things go?

Mitchell (2002) is of the opinion that this unconscious
location of oedipal objects may reproduce our miseries. We
think we are marrying the good parent, but then we find out
that our partner has the qualities we hated in the bad parent.
This could be because the presenting feature of the person
with whom we are about to fall in love often operates as a
defence against its opposite.

Lover beware.

Falling from grace

Why does idealization always have to be paired with de-
idealization. This is not a question, but a lament. Like all
lovers, I wish for the extension of that blissful state of being
held in the loving gaze and arms of someone who really knows
me, understands me, accepts all my faults, always – or at least
whenever I have the time for it. (I'm pretty busy, actually, so I
can't gaze for very long periods of time.)

However, idealization is, unfortunately, often described as
the main *defence mechanism* in couple relationships, as it
makes love "blind" (Dicks, 1967). Because idealization
involves the projection on to the chosen lover of the features
of our ideal image, whether or not he or she actually has these
qualities, it can be seen as defensive. If there is a great deal of
discrepancy between the real person and the ideal, as we come
to know them, then we may have to strain the idealization to
continue it, or else disappointment and devaluation may set in.

As we all know, disappointment is inevitable no matter
how solid our defences seem to be, even though when we are
in the process of falling in love, and trying to maintain this
state, we push this knowledge aside.

"It's so silly. Now I can't even remember why I killed him."

Since love and hate are two sides of a very thin coin, we can understand how even those most in love feel ambivalent about their lover, struggle as they may to keep the negative side of the ambivalence repressed. These intense feelings can, of course, be destructive if they are not discussed, but are acted out.

The fact that the editors of the *New Yorker* magazine knew that both the above cartoon, and the first one in this chapter (see p. 53), would be funny to their millions of readers speaks to everyone's secret knowledge about the intense feelings of hatred and anger that we all experience in close, loving relationships, beginning, of course, with our families of origin.

Altman describes the process of de-idealization in this way:

> In latency and adolescence, love acquires more intensely instinctualized altruistic and self-seeking components – components that war with each other. A little later, in the full flush of the springtime of life, love will surmount all obstacles – nothing must stand in its way. It is a compulsion. For the moment, love for someone other than oneself has the upper hand. Then marriage – husband,

wife, children – puts love to new tests. No small bitterness crops up at the dashing of expectations. The love
object is found to be in default of all those perfections
attributed to it by overestimation – that projection of
one's own narcissism; now, taking inventory, the stock is
found to be short.

(1977, p. 40)

When this happens, especially the first time, often the
reaction is to perceive the now all-too-visible annoying characteristics in the lover as intolerable. If the discrepancy
between how the other actually is and our former idealization
of them is too large and cannot be denied, then we either
have to modify our internal wished-for ideal or we find
ourselves devaluing our lover, sometimes to anyone who will
listen, other than him or her. The devaluation may be motivated by a disappointment that is too painful to bear; by the
need to be the ideal partner by comparison, as in "he's the
bad one, I'm the good one"; or by the fear of our partner
having the same disappointment in us. Sharpe (2000) states
that how partners manage the first sign of a fall from grace
is often predictive of how the relationship will evolve. If
partners' internal ideals are too rigid, then they cannot be
modified to include and integrate an awareness of the other's
faults, and the dreaded devaluation will set in. If a partner is
too accommodating, then they may find themselves in a
relationship that does not nurture them as an individual.

It is at this point that couples often seek help. The first
threat of a landslide of de-idealizations often makes the
partners feel hopeless. *You are not me, you are not who I
thought you were, in fact, I don't know why I married you – I
should have listened to my mother!* For some people, there
were unconscious contradictory wishes involved in the choice
of partner – for example, the wish for mirroring of the self
was opposed to the wish to find the characteristics one lacks.
These contradictions become difficult, if not impossible, for
the other to fulfil. Some individuals, who use splitting as a
defence, in part due to maintaining a representation of one

parent as all good and one as all bad, cannot allow for a grey area – for the idea that we all have our faults and flaws, and that they themselves are not either all perfect or all flawed. For these people, the partner has to be restored to their former idealized state to be lovable.

"What rhymes with 'failed marriage'?"

Despite Fairbairn's observations, many traumatized patients seem to fall in love not with the person who reminds them of their parent, but with the person they hope will heal the wounds the parents have inflicted. To fall in love with the rescuer, or with the person one has rescued, is a frequent theme of romantic love (Bergmann, 1982). This is also, of course, a source of transference and countertransference love. When partners in this situation find that the wounds have not been healed, or that, on the other side of it, they cannot fix another person, they may become angry and begin to feel they are no longer in love.

Some individuals use devaluation as a way of justifying the need to separate. If they can work up a big enough list of defects about their partner, and they do separate, this type of devaluation can operate as a defence against the sadness and pain they feel in the loss of a former loved one.

In the safe haven of a therapeutic environment, couples in the throes of disappointment and de-idealization begin, however tentatively, to be able to acknowledge ambivalent, and even rageful, feelings about the other. As they work their way through and unravel the arguments, they begin to see that both have been victims and both have been agents. "The pain of each is real and requires acknowledgement; the failure of each is real and requires accountability" (Mitchell, 2002, p. 154). With this in mind, they are relieved to find that the mere mention of these feelings usually does not destroy their love, but can lead to helpful exploration and interpretation.

Gail and John met when Gail was a graduate student in John's department. John, a mild and somewhat passive professor, had had two unsuccessful marriages, one to a woman with whom he had two daughters, who was diagnosed with severe bipolar disorder, and one very brief, seemingly reactive, marriage. Gail had never been married, and was an energetic young woman, fifteen years John's junior. Their courtship began with a very exciting affair, while John was extricating himself from his second marriage. John had never had such a young, alive, responsive partner; Gail, who had first idealized John as the all-knowing professor (the teacher–student idealization is probably *almost* as powerful as the therapist–patient idealization), had never had such a caring, loving partner. They decided to marry while they were still in a state of infatuation with each other, and the struggles began soon after. They had two children of their own, in fairly rapid succession, but their most intense battles were over John's daughters, who lived with them because their mother was unable to care for them. One of the complaints this couple presented was that John could not tolerate Gail's rage and intense emotional outbursts, and Gail felt that John was not prepared to act in terms of her difficulties with his children. They were both grieving the loss of the passion that had swept them away in the beginning of their relationship. John, particularly, wanted to paper over the cracks of their fights, in case this, his third marriage, failed; Gail, however, was not letting that happen.

In our work together, John talked about his father, an angry and abusive man, who once locked him in a closet for several hours. His father's rage seemed unpredictable and arbitrary, and John tried hard to be "good" growing up, in an effort to avoid it. The dynamic that seemed most clear with this couple, once both partners could acknowledge how they felt, was that John's lack of responsiveness to Gail's outbursts was based on fear. He was not only frightened of Gail's (*qua* father's) rage, but he was also frightened of his own assertiveness and aggression, which he had projected onto her. This caused Gail to perceive him as weak and ineffectual; the fall from bliss was well in progress when they came for help.

Andrea and Steve, a South African couple in their mid-thirties, came for treatment because of an unwanted pregnancy. They had one planned child, and Steve was having significant work problems. Their courtship had been enhanced by the fact of their both being strangers in a foreign land; they felt like soulmates, with the same longing for a homeland to which neither wanted to return, and because they experienced similar reactions to life in Canada. They were certain their relationship was special because of this. Andrea had a fairly high-paying job, and after they decided to marry, they had their first child within two years. When they started therapy, Steve was taking business courses and had the dream of starting his own lucrative business. He had made two false (and costly) starts when the second pregnancy occurred. The event of the pregnancy had released a tirade of rage from Andrea, who said she wasn't sure she wanted the baby, due to Steve's inability to support the family. They were no longer merged soulmates. They had all but made the decision to abort the pregnancy when their family doctor referred them to me.

This marriage was in a huge crisis – and we had a deadline to meet. In three weeks, it would be too late to decide in favour of abortion. The emotions of both partners were understandably intense in the first two meetings (no history-taking for these two) as I heard from each about the pros and cons of keeping the baby, their projected financial situation, and their anger at each other. Watching Andrea's eyes well up when she touched her stomach and talked about the baby inside her, and indeed watching her body change as time went on, it became impossible for me to remain neutral.

My sense that they both wanted this baby was difficult to sort out from my desire for them not to abort it. I thought it best to share this difficulty with them. The discussion then shifted to Andrea's disappointment in Steve, and how angry she had been over the past year because of his failures at work. She had planned that they should abort the pregnancy because, if the marriage broke up, she would then only have to deal with one child instead of two. Hearing this outpouring of rage and desperation, I thought about the abortion as Andrea's way of punishing Steve, and asked her about this. She began to sob, and agreed. Steve came over to her chair and held her, telling her how much he wanted the baby. They made the final decision to keep the baby after this session.

As our work continued through the pregnancy, Andrea was able to unravel her feelings of anger at Steve which, it turned out, had been instigated by her wealthy father. At one point, Andrea said: "We would never have come here [to therapy] if not for this pregnancy, so I feel like this baby's brought good stuff already." Steve's self-confidence began to improve, and as he felt less like he had to compete with Andrea's father, he began to look for more realistic job opportunities. The reward for all of us was the addition of a bright orange carriage, with a chubby blonde baby girl inside, to our final month of sessions. Their love for each other was beginning to be rekindled, albeit in a more muted light.

Staying in love

To paraphrase Mitchell (2002): love and marriage may go together like a horse and carriage, but it is crucial that the horse of passion be tethered by the rein of reality acceptance to prevent runaways. Lyons (1993) puts it this way: "The task involves the attempt to convert what was originally a largely unconscious, instinctive choice into a conscious commitment. The passion that carried the individuals into the relationship has to be converted into the ongoing energy that will make it work" (pp. 44–45).

When we realize, as Altman states above, that our lover's attributes fall far short of what we wished, and indeed believed, them to be, then the capacity to sustain a love that is neither perfect nor devalued is what is at stake. The transition from "in love" to loving can be a difficult one, especially if early loss or deprivation or incomplete separation from parents are part of the picture. The capacity to make this transition can be only somewhat predictable from the history-taking, based partly on partners' experience of their parents' love for them and for each other, and their parents' marriage. Some individuals have never seen their parents fight, as this was always kept secret from the children, and therefore do not have the idea of reparation, working through, and reconciliation as a natural part of adult relationships. Some individuals' experience of the expression of negative feelings between parents is that it leads to devastating divorce; therefore, they will avoid expressing these feelings at all costs. Partners are also affected, as has been mentioned earlier, by how they themselves have been loved, or not, by early caretakers, the reaction to their perceived deficiencies or misdeeds, and also by parents' reactions to their attempts to separate and mature.

Although the capacity to love over time entails the capacity to tolerate and repair hatred, hatred is not all there is when the climate changes. Disappointment may be just that, and the role of the couples therapist can be to help couples understand why the disappointment has come about. That no one can live up to an individual's concept of the perfect lover, even though we enjoy the idea that we might, may have to be explained to the partners. As well, understanding the choice of partner in the light of one's background, knowing something about the tendency we all have to use projection, and acknowledging the inner push to repeat old patterns, as discussed earlier in this chapter, can all be extremely helpful, in terms of knowing what to do when reality sets in.

Freud (1912) characterized "a completely normal attitude in love" as the confluence of "two currents," the *"tender and the sensual"* (italics mine). People who cannot desire where they love or love where they desire have become derailed in their development. To be able to experience tender affection and sexual desire with the same person at the same time is, therefore, a highly difficult achievement – for both men and women – and seems to be, quite frankly, an indication of growing up.

Well before Freud, in 1643, John Milton published his *Doctrine & Discipline of Divorce*, an essay addressed to members of the English parliament. In defending divorce, Milton also offered his thinking on what a long-term, committed relationship should consist of. (His own first, unhappy marriage may have contributed to his formulation.) He wrote: "In God's intention, a meet and happy conversation is the chiefest and noblest end of marriage" (cited in Mead, 2003). Milton's understanding of the word *conversation* (derived from the Latin verb *conversari*: to live together) would have been a broad one, encompassing not only meaningful talk, but an easy intimacy.

In this excerpt from D.H. Lawrence's novel *Women in Love*, Ursula and Birkin have achieved this, at least for the moment:

> She clung nearer to him. He held her close, and kissed her softly, gently. It was such peace and heavenly freedom, just to fold her and kiss her gently, and not to have any thoughts or any desires or any will, just to be still with her, to be perfectly still and together, in a peace that was not sleep, but content in bliss. To be content in bliss, without desire or insistence anywhere, this was heaven: to be together in happy stillness.
>
> (Lawrence, 2002 [1920], p. 261)

Can the ability to integrate passion into loving and sustain it past the eruption of anger and negative feelings be learned, or improved upon, in the environment of couples therapy? This, we all know, is a tall order, and some analytic thinkers say it cannot be done. "Full face-to-face erotic intimacy is too blinding, like looking directly at the sun, for people who have been raised on a diet of emotional scarcity" (Miller, 1995, p. 113).

Mitchell (2002), who has been cited earlier in this chapter, entitled his final book *Can love last? The fate of romance over time*, which should have made it an instant best-seller. His answer to the first part of the title is: yes, but – passion cannot. Mitchell maintains that our needs for safety and passion are conflicting, since deadness is a requirement for security. "Passionlessness in long-term relationships is often a consequence not of the extinguishing of a flame but of collusive efforts to keep the relationship inert in a sodden stasis" (Mitchell, 2002, p. 55). What is so dangerous about desiring someone you love, according to Mitchell, is that you can lose him or her; therefore, we may even consciously or unconsciously find ourselves inhibiting the excitement we felt for our partner earlier on.

Is this the good news? Could we really feel passionate about our partner if only we weren't so worried about the loss of a secure relationship? In a way, this seems contradictory to what we think we know, that is, that a healthy relationship can mature over time and that many people, after many years together, *can* have a love that at least sometimes includes passion, whether on a holiday, or a date night, or just in genuine appreciation of the other. The appreciation may grow out of their shared history – sometimes by having survived a difficult or, indeed, a pleasurable time together, sometimes by feeling proud of what the couple have accomplished as a partnership, or sometimes even by comparing themselves to other couples they know and feeling grateful for having each other.

The capacity for mature love, for moving from intense infatuation to tender affection and appreciation, is related to

"Come a little bit closer. You're my kind of man."

the capacity for mature object relations in general, in other words, a sufficient degree of ego development; both can be affected by therapeutic treatment. When partners are at extreme ends of a continuum – for example, to oversimplify: "good–bad" in the case of Anne and Michael – then helping them to move closer to each other and to see how each possesses the potential for both qualities can lead to their having a more mature, accepting perception of the other.

Berkowitz (1999) states that although the literature emphasizes the neurotic fit we often see in couples, there is also a healthy potential in relationships to master a previously bad and frustrating object relationship. In one couple I saw, the male partner had grown up with an inconsistent mother who arbitrarily doled out smothering love and humiliating punishment, seemingly unconnected to any behaviour of his. His parents had an angry divorce when he was 11 years of age and, in their continued acrimony, made use of him and his siblings for their own needs to express hostility to each other. This man chose a relationship with a woman from a steadily loving and caring family. Although it was not her conscious intention to "cure" him, she did – by being consistent and present even though he was, for a long time, unable to make an acknowledged commitment to her. He used work and an interest in sports to take himself away from her; she stayed with him, however, offering good-enough attunement to his needs, and he was eventually able to love and appreciate her in an intensely genuine way. After ten years of living together, they were married. When they came for therapy, it was to discuss problems with a hyperactive child.

As in Kohut's description of the effect of the repair of empathic failures when they occur between analyst and analysand, the repair of failures in the empathic fabric of a couple's relationship can strengthen the bond between the two individuals.

In some way, the rest of this book is devoted to the subject of staying in love: helping couples tolerate and be patient with each other, forgive each other and themselves, better understand their partner's needs and motivations and better communicate their own, and to increase their capacity to appreciate and enjoy each other. Another tall order.

Chapter 4

The ongoing therapy: technique

"Forty-one years of marriage. That's a long, long, long learning curve."

The transition from the history-taking session to the ongoing therapy is usually not a difficult one for couples. Unlike in individual treatment, where the patient may find the history-taking an easy, structured, ice-breaker, most couples are champing at the bit to get started.

If the therapist has never worked with more than one individual at a time (i.e. no group or family therapy experience), the task ahead can seem daunting. It's not that *all* the ways of thinking about patients and relating to them in individual therapy have to be put aside, just most of them. Then they can be reintegrated as one gets to know the couple better. This is not individual therapy times two: it is a whole different ballgame. Because there is so much happening in each moment, the therapist is always on the lookout for who's doing what to whom and why. Seeing couples on a relatively long-term basis allows for a deeper understanding of these dynamics.

In this chapter, I have divided the ongoing therapy into beginning and middle phases. Obviously these phases will overlap, as the partners move around in their work together. Termination (Chapter 7), as well, is not a clearly delimited phase – just as in individual treatment. The subsections used here are an attempt to organize the almost unorganizable. I have offered a detailed description of the actual work with two couples, but have also included examples from other couples to elaborate points.

The opening phase

In the opening phase of the treatment, after the history-taking sessions, I inform the couple that I will no longer take notes, and that they can talk about whatever they feel is significant and, as much as possible, whatever is on their mind. They know from the previous sessions that they will both have a chance to speak and react, as they have already had some experience of my watching for this. Often one partner will begin immediately, by (a) complaining about the other, (b) reporting an incident that has just happened, or (c) volunteering the other, as in: "Why don't you start?" I may have thoughts about all three of these possibilities – for example, (a) the person wants me to see how bad things are for them; (b) the person is ready to use the sessions to work on real examples; and (c) the person is scared to talk, avoids being assertive, and puts their partner on the spot. However, I do not give those kinds of observations at this point. As in individual work, first and foremost, I am trying to establish a rapport with both partners. Therefore I tend to go along with however they open, and "file" my thoughts for offering to them at a later time, especially if these ways of relating to each other seem to be part of a pattern. The therapist has to keep in mind that, even though they seem ready to begin – each in his or her own way – still the couple as a unit may fear exposing their secret bonds, the emotional underbelly of the relationship, which is often embarrassing to both. Knowing this, it is interesting to watch for joint (collusive) and individual defences.

Although balancing airtime is an important consideration, in exceptional circumstances, when one partner has a great deal to say about an issue, or when one partner is under extreme stress for relational or individual reasons, they may have the floor for a longer period of time in one session, or even for the whole session. An example of this will follow. I always acknowledge that this is happening, and ensure that the other partner is on side. It is generally understood that things will be more balanced in the next session.

The therapist's identifying more with one partner than the other deserves a mention here and will be discussed in detail in the chapter on countertransference. This can happen very quickly – even from the first telephone call. We may easily relate to one partner, feel sorry for one, find one totally unlikeable – it is human nature. These feelings must be noticed by the therapist, as they will certainly be noticed by the couple. Of course each therapist has their own conscious and unconscious agenda, often to do with making a silk purse out of what is sometimes a sow's ear; being as aware as possible of one's agenda is what is important.

In the opening phase, there is, usefully, a honeymoon period, which usually consists of an idealizing transference to the therapist by one or both partners. This works to establish a safe environment and to encourage the telling of terrible stories.

It can at least be said that couples who continue to live in states of severe conflict and mutual frustration, have not given up the struggle to work-through and come to terms with, their deeper object worlds . . . . It is the defusion of ambivalence which allows the partners to communicate their primitive, unfillable love needs to each other in heavily disguised or oblique ways: by sulks, revenge, in short by every device of "representation by the opposite." Such fireworks and suffering demonstrate the liveness of the deeper libidinal involvement.

(Dicks, 1967, p. 85)

"We had an argument, and now he's trying to make me feel bad."

As these stories are elaborated, both individuals begin to see that they can talk about issues in the therapy they never thought they would be able to describe to anyone. The general decibel level gets lowered and there is an increasing atmosphere of calm, provided by the presence and tone of the therapist, in which partners can begin to hear each other again. One couple described my role at this point as "translating" what one partner has said to the other.

There are times, although not often in my experience, when the disclosure of a partner's ambivalent feelings leads to rigid defensiveness on the part of the other and irreparable damage. It is the task of the couples therapist to assess the readiness of *each* partner to hear complaints, and then to contain the hatred and hopelessness in a manner that makes it more workable, if that is, indeed, what both partners want. The word "each" is in italics above as a reminder that, all through the therapy, individual partners may be at different levels of narcissistic vulnerability, psychological growth, psychological mindedness, and ability to tolerate input that may be negative.

Chantal and Brad: opening phase

Chantal and Brad (the engineers introduced earlier, who came for treatment after the disclosure of Chantal's affair) had revealed many important critical incidents, that is, turning-points, in their histories to date, some of which were mentioned in Chapter 2.

Their early courtship was described as "wonderfully smooth"; Chantal had just ended a stormy relationship and when she met Brad she saw him as a breath of fresh air. He had all the qualities she wanted in a husband: he played sports; he wasn't intense; she never felt scared or anxious with him. They were married after two years. Chantal said she was not swept off her feet, but felt safe with him; Brad, for his part, was smitten, "I fell madly in love with her." About five years and one baby into the marriage, while Chantal was finishing her Ph.D. in their hometown of Vancouver, she was offered a teaching job in Boston. Brad liked the job he had, and did not want to move. This was when the arguing began, and Chantal reported that Brad became very cold. They did move to Boston and, as was mentioned earlier, Brad was able eventually to get a job, but it involved a fair amount of travel. Their relationship became more distant and Chantal pushed for a second child, mainly to keep her company. After two years, and another baby, they both wanted to return to Canada. Chantal secured a university teaching position and Brad was hired by the largest engineering firm in the country; they moved to a suburb of Toronto with their two young children. About six months later, Chantal began an affair with a respected colleague. I heard all this information in pieces from each of them over the first few sessions.

At the start of our work together, Chantal and Brad moved away from the history-taking quickly, as if to indicate that they wanted to get on with the real business at hand. Chantal, who cried through most of the beginning sessions, stated, by the fifth session, that she was sure she wanted to live apart from Brad, even though the extra-marital relationship was definitely over. Brad did not want this to happen.

"Things are heating up," I wrote in my notes in their second month of treatment. *"C. is insistent on moving out and has been actively looking for a place to live. B. just won't give up – keeps saying he loves her. Since he can't communicate his rage in any other way, he has begun to somatize, and is worried about his blood pressure, which he reports has gone 'sky high.' I asked if he would like a referral for individual counselling, thinking he may need extra support and a place to express his anger away from C., and I am getting concerned about his health. He said 'No, but maybe when she moves out' – which now seems inevitable. I will offer them some sessions – regularly or periodically – after they separate. He's now using the children as his main emotional attachment and support – but she's taking them away for 10 days during my holiday."*

A few weeks after this was written, the decision was made for Chantal to lease an apartment downtown, near the university, and she moved out, leaving Brad with the children in their home. This was done for expediency, as one of Chantal's complaints about their lifestyle had been the hour-long commute downtown to her work. Brad loved suburban living: he worked in their large garden and was involved in the children's school. Chantal preferred city life. The arrangement they worked out was that time with the children would be split by Chantal living in the downtown apartment most of the week, and Brad living there for the rest of the week. The children remained at home with whichever parent was there, and seemed to adjust to this. They were told that their mother was working on a project at the university and needed to live close by some of the time, and since they were used to their father having to travel, they apparently assumed he was travelling when he was living downtown. On weekends, they were both usually home with the children, which gave them the chance to talk. They both asked to continue weekly couples therapy, and neither wanted individual treatment.

Mirella and Nick: opening phase

Mirella and Nick, the Italian "odd couple" (in their differing needs for orderliness), also introduced to the reader in Chapter 2, had presented with Mirella's fear of Nick's anger. Mirella's conscious but unspoken agenda for treatment had been: *I'm OK, he's got a rage problem, but he'd never go into therapy alone, so I came with him.* Mirella's family was described as having "no conflict, very soft, my parents didn't discipline us." Nick's father was described as "domineering; he yells." He also disciplined the children by hitting them with a belt. Both his parents were described as "fearful and worry warts." As has been mentioned, Mirella and Nick had been married for ten years when I met them, and had two young children. I have seen them for two years so far.

The opening phase of their treatment centred on Nick's anger concerning the household mess, and Mirella's lack of discipline of their two young children. Mirella stated that Nick yelled at the children which frightened her; Nick stated that Mirella undid what he had said by over-coddling them, which got him enraged again. In a typical early session, Mirella began crying because of a fight they had that morning. Nick admitted he "badgered" her (there was no report of physical violence), and acknowledged that he stored up ammunition against her. The reason he had to store it up, he said, was because he was not allowed to say anything negative to Mirella, or she would "overreact." Mirella actually did look like she was scared of Nick in the early sessions, and he did put her down. Nick complained: "She gets mad if I tell her she's stupid." I said: "I'd get mad if you told me *I* was stupid." Then he said: "Well, I don't really mean 'stupid,' I mean she's not doing things in the right order." This type of conversation was frequent, with all of us trying to find ways for Nick to express himself that would not be experienced as a denigration by Mirella.

As far as I could tell in the beginning, both wanted the marriage to work, even though Mirella had a habit of playing the separation card when things got rough. She was like a kid threatening to run away from home, with no plan and no viable means of support. Still, it had the effect she hoped for – it got Nick's attention by inducing a fear of abandonment, and this led to her seeing how much he didn't want her to leave.

It is in this phase that while the therapist is assessing the couple, both partners, are, of course, assessing the therapist. (Does this therapist really understand us? Does the therapist like him/her better? Why did the therapist say we walk on eggshells with each other – I didn't like that, etc.) These initial individual and joint assessments can help facilitate the treatment, or be used to derail it later. There is jockeying for position – sometimes literally. It is interesting how some couples always sit in the same seats, and some change around. Norms about lateness are also observable, as are attempts to prolong the session. Transferences and countertransferences begin immediately, and can be very intense.

The middle phase

In the middle phase, I start sessions with the question: "So, how are things?" I look at each of them, and then one partner starts: by reporting an incident that has just happened; picking up on something from the last session; or bringing in a relatively new topic. We all listen, and then if the other partner has not already responded, I invite him or her to do so. This topic may take up the whole session, or lead to other issues we have talked about before. It may happen that one individual gets into the habit, at this stage, of giving a report card on how the other behaved that week. This is done with the fantasy that the therapist colludes with their method of rating "improvement," and therefore has to be commented on by the therapist.

During this phase, I often take the time to re-read the family histories. Because couples usually don't continue to talk about their past and their growing-up life the way individuals do, it is somewhat more difficult to remember family details. Once the therapy starts moving, the focus is often on contemporary life, and it is easy to forget details from the historical context.

The couple usually move from trying to impress or compete for the therapist (the honeymoon is over) to digging deeper into the issues for which they came into treatment.

Interpretation is an important part of the middle phase. For over 100 years, interpretation has been seen as the main form of therapeutic action in psychoanalysis and psychoanalytic psychotherapy, and was originally defined as making the unconscious conscious. According to classical theory, an interpretation is offered by the analyst to the analysand to help bring the latent content of a dream or free association to the surface so that patients are better informed about their unconscious conflicts and motivations. Currently, even in psychoanalysis, patients themselves often give interpretations, and the focus is not always on the unconscious; in contemporary psychoanalysis, interpretation is a process which is mutually contributed to.

This tool for expanding understanding is very useful in work with couples, and can help partners to know more about the puzzling – sometimes unconscious – meanings in the troubled interaction. Interpretations may or may not be around transference, but can involve one individual's conscious or unconscious contribution to the conflict (e.g. in the case of Andrea's need to punish Steve by contemplating aborting a pregnancy), or they can be focused on the inter-action of the couple as a whole (e.g. in the case of Rita and Stan, where their blaming mode was a collusive defence against feared intimacy). Interpretations offered with both partners present are amazingly productive.

Interpretation, like other forms of observation in couples therapy, is usually not delivered from the perspective of the therapist as authority, but is co-constructed with the couple; often, once they get the hang of it, couples, who have a richer source of knowledge about their families and their relation-ship than we do, offer interpretations of their partner's and their own behaviours in a remarkably helpful manner. Because of the mutuality involved, the therapist can hear his or her hypotheses validated or shot down; sometimes one partner can help the other to make sense of, or accept, an interpretation. If all goes well, everyone feels more com-fortable in this phase, and a genuine partnership emerges with all three participants joining in to modify an interpretation or insight that may have been initiated by any one in the triad.

There are times, in this phase, when one partner may attempt to act as a *"co-therapist,"* not only identifying with the therapist and separating him- or herself from the "troubled" partner, but in a genuine wish to practise new skills and to help the other. In the example of Lisa and Eric, described in Chapter 1, where we spent some time on Lisa's difficulties with her mother, Eric, aligning himself with me, explained to Lisa how separation is an "attitude" and doesn't mean cutting yourself off emotionally completely from your parents, as Lisa imagined she would have to do. He felt he had accomplished this with his father who had previously been a negative focus of his professional life, as he had wanted to prove to him that he could succeed in business without his help. His anger at not being recognized as competent had been a prime motivator for his own hard work. Eric stated that he no longer cared if his father knew how successful he was. He spent his time with him in other ways – and probably loved his father more. He explained this in an intense tone, and kept

saying to me: "Why doesn't Lisa get this stuff about separation?" At one point I expressed: "OK. Everyone on Lisa!" as
that was what I felt was happening.

In the very next session, Eric declared that he would not
attend a party held by Lisa's parents, as he was still very angry
at them for the way they had behaved toward him – a new
incident had occurred two weeks' previously – and this was a
chance to express it, i.e. by staying home. "Now you're having
trouble separating from my parents," Lisa said. "Why can't
you just go and enjoy the party with the people there who we
like? Separation is an 'attitude.'"

There is a different example of the "co-therapist" phe-
nomenon in the case of Gail and John – discussed more fully
in the next chapter on transference – where John and I
became the "parents" and Gail was the "child." This can
emerge as an extension of the dynamics already present within
the couple.

When the co-therapist situation happens during the middle
phase, I usually make the observation, and sometimes I am
able to interpret it in the context of the therapy. There are
times when I don't comment: it depends on how often it
occurs; how the other partner reacts to it; and whether the
other partner gets a chance to do the same – which can
demonstrate that they are learning to help each other outside
of the sessions. I never (consciously) encourage it.

Silences, although not as frequent or as lengthy as in individual therapy, still occur in couples therapy. Once everyone
is less anxious, a silence may indicate reflection on a comment; or that one partner is having trouble speaking about
an issue and is using the silence to formulate their thoughts;
or that one or the other or both are feeling completely
resistant to discussing a particular topic, or to being in
therapy at all; or that one or both are angry at the therapist.
As in individual therapy, silences can be a useful source of
information. If the silence does not feel like a natural part of
the "flow," I comment on it and ask about its purpose.

Since some of the initial crises have been resolved during the
middle phase, or are under productive discussion, the

underlying dynamics in the relationship begin to stare us all in the face. For example, often partners discover that they have been taking roles that place them on extreme ends of one or more continua: parent–child, good guy–bad guy, socializer–hermit, orderly one–messy one. The roles are usually not totally conscious when a couple come for treatment. They are a combination of projective identifications, idealizations, narcissistic vulnerabilities, transferences from early object relations, fears, and wishes. The polarization of roles or affect can come about because the collusive need to exaggerate one feature of a partner's personality is seen as "beneficial" to keeping the relationship going, or sometimes because one partner is attempting to correct the excesses of the other by a kind of role modelling. If one, for example, feels the other is too outgoing, he or she may become quieter as a way of saying: "Calm down." The other partner, however, may become even more outgoing, as a way of saying: "Why can't you liven up? See?"

In the case of an unconscious contract, as in *I need to be taken care of – Taking care of people is what I have to offer in a relationship*, then things can go smoothly for a long time. One partner can evoke the complementary response in the other, especially if the other is primed from past experience to respond. Sandler (1976) calls this role-responsiveness when it occurs between therapist and patient, the patient needing to impose and experience a role-relationship as a vehicle to gratification. The analyst, Sandler says, may have a tendency to reflexively accept the role that the patient is forcing on him or her. In the same way, partners will accept roles forced onto each other, usually ones that fit or that allow them to avoid flexing a part of their psychic muscle that has remained atrophied for years.

In the case of Chantal and Brad, she was the bad guy, he was the good guy. Once this is noticed, I usually appeal to each partner to think about their own need to be more in the position of the other. "Isn't it boring," I may ask, "to always be the good/bad one?" In the case of Brad, because he was so worried about being identified with his father who had an affair that was known to the family, I said: "Haven't you taken this good-guy thing a little far? We can see how hard you've been trying to not be like him, but what happened to your badness – your need for passion, for spontaneity, for taking risks?" Chantal was able to look at her need to be seen as good, at least some of the time – not as the happy homemaker, but as a loving parent and also as a loving wife, which she had always wanted herself to be.

I often ask partners to imagine if they could each come in a little toward the middle from their extreme ends of the continuum without losing their charm or their attraction to each other. The possibility that one or both do not want to change these dynamics can now be considered.

As this phase moves along, couples usually begin to communicate in a more satisfying manner outside of the sessions and are able to make better and better use of their time in therapy. They are more interested in talking to *each other* rather than complaining, and interestingly, rather than addressing the therapist. Partners also learn that they can talk about the most minute details of ordinary life (e.g. loading the dishwasher) and see how these serve as examples of their interactions at home. As more of an understanding of the dynamics underlying the problems emerges, the therapist may be able to offer a different model of an interaction that might have addressed the needs of both partners better than the one that got them into a fight. I sometimes do this in an exaggerated manner, which has the effect of helping the couple see where things went askew, under a magnifying glass, and also makes them laugh, so the medicine goes down easier.

It is interesting how frequently *dreams* are brought into the therapy. Because couples are usually not told that dreams are of interest here, as patients may be in individual treatment, the dreams are brought in spontaneously, as it were, when the partners get more involved in this approach to the work. In this milieu the relationship itself, along with the therapeutic relationship, becomes an arena for expressing and hearing this additional layer of rich unconscious relational material. One partner's dream may be a way for them to communicate with the other and with the therapist. The dream can express unconscious wishes and fears, and allow for the opportunity to hear free associative material from both individuals. I usually ask the dreamer for their associations first, as one would do in individual therapy, and then get their partner's response. The co-interpretations – often of even the latent content – can be fascinating and extremely fruitful. Of course, if the therapist gets too excited when a dream is brought, then dreams can become a source of competition between the partners. Often couples report that the telling of dreams to each other outside of the therapy has become a pleasurable experience, particularly when they have learned to free associate and not make judgements.

In both the middle phase and the ending phase of treatment (Chapter 7), the question may arise as to how much *individual therapy* can be done, if one person is actually in need, during the couples treatment. The following considerations must then be taken into account: (1) Time lost versus time gained: the amount of airtime taken by one individual can erode the couple's therapy time and may cause resentment. However, time can be gained for the troubled individual because a known therapeutic relationship has already been established; time can be gained for the couple because the partner being present during the work can contribute to a deeper understanding of the difficulties of the other, and can also be helpful in offering interpretations. (2) The feeling in the room: if there is considerable mistrust and hostility between the partners, then, of course, the one who seems in need may be concerned that any disclosures will be used "against" them, for example, brought up in an argument. Therefore, to protect this partner, it would be better to refer him or her to an individual therapist. (3) The content and intensity of the issue: does it look like an acute issue that will be eased by the individual talking about it in the somewhat compromised airtime available, or is longer-term treatment needed; is the content related at all to the couple's relationship? (4) The collusion on the part of the couple, and possibly the therapist, to use the individual issues as a resistance to, or at least distraction from, what may be very painful couples work: this could be analysed, in part, by noticing what the content of the joint therapy has been just preceding the revelation of an individual issue. (5) The possible interpretation of a referral: the upset partner may feel rejected by the couples therapist's referral to an outside therapist, or may see it as proof that they really are the problem in the relationship; the other partner may also see this as evidence of their partner's greater psychological issues, and hence believe that they are the more stable, i.e. better, one in the relationship. Bringing in individual issues often occurs once the relationship crises have cooled down, and, interestingly, can sometimes be an indication that things are actually going more smoothly between the partners.

Chantal and Brad: middle phase

Four months into therapy, Chantal began one of our sessions with this dream:

> I dreamt that Brad was working on a very important bridge linking the west to the east. He put these huge stones on the structure which looked like it couldn't support it. In the end, they found out that it wasn't Brad's fault – someone else had done it.

Since they were not living together at this time, Chantal had not communicated the dream to Brad, and so it was fresh in the session. I asked first for Chantal's associations. "I don't know. Brad usually doesn't work on bridges, at least not real ones. I think I'm feeling guilty. I'm the one who caused this whole problem." Brad said: "Yah. But you see me as putting the burden on the structure. So maybe I'm the guilty one." Sometimes there is a free-for-all of free associations, which I join with my own. In this case, since there were few associations from the couple, my contribution was about the timing of this dream, which I thought spoke to Chantal's attempt to understand what had happened between them, which I felt (optimistically) was very much on her mind. In my private associations, I imagined that Chantal was feeling burdened by Brad in general – his need to have her as the suburban wife, and his lack of attunement to her more intense emotions. Her reference to east and west seemed to me to be referring to their earlier happy beginnings in the west, which Brad seemed to be straining to impose on their life here. I also wondered if there was a transference meaning (or two) in the dream, my first association being that Chantal might be worried that the therapy wasn't strong enough to hold and help them.

I raised my associations slowly in subsequent sessions and encouraged them to join me. The therapist's giving too many possible interpretations of a dream at first with couples, as with individuals, especially when there is a poverty of associations, leads to the bringing in of dreams for the purpose of having the therapist express what the individual cannot, or for the therapist to explain to the dreamer or their partner what is really going on. Of course, it may also have the effect of shutting down both partners' own imaginative associations, which are often very different from the therapist's. We referred back to Chantal's dream periodically.

Several months into treatment, Chantal reported to us that a graduate student in her department had been sexually molested by a faculty member that week and had come to her for help. She seemed very agitated, and so I asked her to say more about this. I knew, from a brief mention in our second session, that she herself had been the victim of ongoing sexual abuse by a paternal uncle from when she was a young child until puberty, and that her parents had both refused to believe her that this was, indeed, the case. Brad had always known this. Never having had the opportunity to express the feelings that were stored up inside her about her own abuse in a *therapeutic* climate, Chantal began to sob convulsively as she spoke about it. Here was an instance of the necessity to focus on an individual issue. This had certainly been a critical incident in Chantal's life, with obvious important residual effects. Although I was aware that there would be an effect on Brad and on the relationship as a result of working with

Chantal individually, I judged that it would be beneficial overall. A patient of mine whom I knew well, was in need of help, and I spent the rest of the session (about three-quarters of it) listening to, and trying to help Chantal express the details of that terrible time. In the back of my mind was the possibility of referring her for individual treatment, if I thought that we could not do the work in these sessions.

In this situation, the issue of sexual abuse was highly relevant and the atmosphere in the room was conducive to all of us contributing together; in addition, Chantal's distress seemed somewhat circumscribed, and she was probably not in need of a referral. This was not a resistance but constituted a deepening of our attempts to understand and heal.

As Chantal talked over a number of sessions, Brad first became involved by filling in for me the details of her family life that were connected to this trauma. After this, as he listened, he became her outraged saviour, which took them back to one of the dynamics that was evident when they first fell in love. We discovered that Brad, with his clean-cut image, had seemed to Chantal to be a potential healer of that dark time. This role now also gave Brad more confidence in himself and in his participation in the therapy, all of which we acknowledged.

One of the most immediately beneficial results of this individual work – carried out over several weeks – besides helping Chantal to unburden herself of the anguish and guilt related to this period, was that Brad understood better why there were problems in their sexual life. As things had been deteriorating between them, he had been pressing for more sexual contact as a way of reassuring himself about their love. This had caused Chantal to become angry and pull away. Leading up to the affair, and for months after it, she did not want any sexual contact with him; this had happened previously, for extended periods of time, during their relationship. Whenever Chantal had pulled back, Brad had moved in, making himself more offensive to her.

As well, we came to understand that when the love affair had started it was reminiscent of the "illicit sex" of the earlier abuse. One of the attractions for Chantal was that this was real love, with a mature man, who was enthralled with her but did not need to live with her. Brad, whom she had known since university, seemed to be a boy by comparison. The secrecy of their meetings, highly sexually exciting at first, had given her a chance to act out the guilty excitement of the abuse. Another draw of the affair was that Chantal could enact the split between sexual desire and long-term committed love, which had been an ongoing issue in relationships for her – fuelled by the conflicted experience of the uncle's abuse.

Brad's initial idealization of Chantal when they were dating had made her feel good about herself for the first time. Now, however, he was being experienced as a dull burden, as she said later in referring back to her dream. She felt trapped with him and their suburban lifestyle. She was also beginning to think that Brad could not survive on his own, that he needed her talents for cooking, socializing with friends, and parenting to make his life happy. He did not have any friends separate from their relationship, and depended on her for most of their life outside of work. She convinced herself that he did not really love her; he was with her because he did not want to be alone.

In this couple's therapy a great deal was out in the open, starting with the earlier sexual abuse, and importantly, the affair – when and how it started, and Chantal's reaction to its ending. This is not always the case with couples who have been involved in an extra-marital relationship. However, in this situation, we were free to make interpretations about the link between the affair and the earlier abuse; to talk about Chantal's search for a reliable father; and to acknowledge that Brad's nightmare had come true, as he connected it to his father's affair. To his credit, Brad was even able to consider his possible contribution to an enactment. When there is not as much shared information in the treatment, then naturally comments and hypotheses are more limited.

Seven months into the treatment: *"Things are going ok, at least B. is straining to make them ok. He really feels he has grown through this, and he does seem to be communicating with C. better. Last session seemed to help where he said, rather self-pityingly – 'I guess I've been a lousy communicator' and I said – 'So it seems.' Made him laugh, but I think he got it. They both have said they want the relationship to continue. He still has trouble being overtly angry at her. After our work on the sexual abuse, he's too scared to tell her he's enraged – doesn't want to upset the apple cart – and may see her as more fragile."*

After this session, we talked about how angry Brad must be about the affair and his difficulty in expressing this to Chantal. He kept saying, "I'm dealing with it," meaning in his head. He was terrified that expressing his anger would wreak havoc on a still precarious situation. I pushed a little by saying it for him: "How *could* you?" I asked, looking at Chantal. She replied that she didn't want an affair, but realized that she had been looking for something more ever since Brad had been "too emotionally involved" with one of her students in Boston. This was news to me, so I turned to Brad, and said: "How could *you*?" Brad said he thought he was helping this young woman who was away from home, and looking to him for advice. He appeared to be unaware that this woman was developing a crush on him (and probably he on her) and that, in a way, he had strayed first. Although this obviously could not account for all that had happened after, it opened up a new dimension on the issue. There followed a productive conversation *between the two of them* about how their relationship had stopped meeting needs of both partners, and why. Critical incidents relating to various periods during their time in Boston were discussed in more detail.

Ten months into the therapy: *"Things seem to be getting better. They've resumed a sexual relationship – spending all weekends together. B. hates the downtown apartment, and was relieved when I encouraged him to use that word. C. loves it. She loves having the space and being close to work. They talked about building a space for her in their house. She's actually missing him when they're not together."*

As the resentment and hatred on both parts were somewhat eased, they began to raise concerns about their children, not only regarding the disruption of having parents coming and going, but also regarding the differences in how they disciplined the children. This was an indication that they were able to turn their attention away from the recent intense conflict, at least for the moment, and also showed that they knew they could use the therapy to talk about any problems they had. With their improved ability to communicate, and to think about issues in a more psychological manner, they worked at trying to understand the effects of their behaviour and the differences in their parenting styles on the children.

During this time, Brad enrolled in cooking classes and genuinely enjoyed his increasing ability to cook good meals. He was becoming the happy homemaker he had needed Chantal to be, and indulging his identification with his mother. Thanksgiving was approaching and he planned to cook the entire meal for Chantal, their children, and one other couple. His excitement was so palpable I couldn't stop myself from asking for his stuffing recipe! The icing on the cake came, as luck would have it, just after this time, when each of them was honoured in their professions. Brad was invited to be a Vice President and Chantal was nominated for a prestigious national award.

Chantal and Brad's story will be continued in the chapter on termination.

Mirella and Nick: middle phase

This phase with this couple went on for years, without much progress – at least that is how it felt to all of us. A great deal of time was spent on the running of the household: Nick's need for order, and Mirella's need to do many things at once. Mirella acknowledged she felt overwhelmed by the number of household tasks, and that she rarely finished one before another urgently presented itself. They took turns occupying the high ground. Nick would say: "If you would just hang up clothes and put away shoes and toys when you come in, I'd be able to get into the house without stepping on stuff. As it is, I can't even get in my own front door." When Mirella had the high ground, she would say: "I can't live with his anger any more; he has crossed a line."

Six months into it, my notes read: "*Things seem to be staying the same or getting worse. M., who is having extreme difficulty, keeps giving ultimatums re: N.'s 'yelling.' N. says he doesn't yell. This discrepancy is probably partly due to the difference in emotional environments growing up. Also N. needs to maintain a 'macho' image, as he acknowledges, defending against his smothering mother. Maybe they need to keep this up. Same complaints every week. N. maintains that M. won't look at her part in it and totally blames him in here.*"

"I'm not yelling at you, I'm yelling with you."

This was another situation (similar to that of Anne and Michael, the lawyers mentioned in Chapter 1) where I acted as a container for an intense emotion, again anger, processed it, and gave it back to Nick, and indirectly, to Mirella; again, it was obvious to both of them that I was not afraid of Nick. I had heard the "yelling." He did indeed raise his voice, but there was no evidence of hatred or potential violence in it.

Actually, I liked Nick a lot: I appreciated his intelligence, his efforts at trying to make things better, his insight, and his sense of humour. In this case, my approach with each of them, observed by the other, provided a model for acceptance and empathy.

One of the avenues we took during this phase was to explore Mirella's picture of what I was now seeing as a suspiciously no-conflict family. Why was she so sensitive to fighting? What was Nick evoking from her early experience that was so traumatic? But even Nick agreed with Mirella's description of her family, and referred to her father as a "pussycat." Since there appeared to be no reason for him to collude with her at this point, I took him at his word. "Maybe someone else in the family scared her," he suggested. Mirella could think of no one. Dead end.

Desperate, I abandoned my psychoanalytic stance and tried a role play with them, asking each of them to play the part of the other and to express the other's point of view. The best part of this exercise was that it was hilarious. Mirella had a good sense of humour, too; they took the roles completely empathically, and were even able to imitate perfectly the voice of the other person. Each was able to laugh at hearing how they sounded, and agreed that their partner had hit it right on. Other than providing some comic relief, however, this did not advance us as much as I had hoped. They already knew that the other would be able to do this accurately, and were not as impressed as I was with their performances. The only benefit it seemed I could offer them was to relate it to their problems with their children who, of course, also knew who was "soft" and who was "harsh," and were making as good use of it as their latency-aged skills allowed. I suggested they fool the kids by switching these roles for a day or two and see what happened. They were intrigued with this idea and tried it.

As time went on, Nick was the one who complained more about Mirella, saying he felt judged by her, that she whined a lot at him, and that he didn't think she was "looking in the mirror." Had I bought Mirella's agenda that the problem

was Nick's anger, even though I consciously had such positive feelings towards Nick? When the opportunity presented
itself regarding Nick's "yelling," I said to Mirella, "Well, you
didn't choose a milquetoast for a partner, did you?" She
agreed that such a type would not be attractive to her. She
then said that even though she didn't know why, she knew
she was overly sensitive to any anger. As if hearing this for
the first time, Nick was able to acknowledge that his angry
tone could be ratcheted down a notch or two. Mirella ended
this session by spontaneously listing qualities in Nick that she
appreciated.

Four months later: "*M. was late – and we were off to the
races. When this happens, N. says he doesn't want to be here
(although he's really into it in the session), but he makes the
effort to come on time. He's mad at her for 'always' being late.
She says it's only sometimes, etc. Discussion re: M.'s disorganization, but it turns out that N., who probably has at least
mild OCD, is disorganized in his own way. I watched them
fight for a few minutes, and noticed that M. is much less scared
of N. She had emailed him at work about the agenda for
tonight! – this is a new one for me – never thought of it.*"

Things were finally starting to move. Mirella took some
time in a session to tentatively describe herself as being
unable to say "no" to items assigned to her at work. As I
asked her more about this, I heard that she could not finish
tasks at work, either. She then acknowledged that she felt
overwhelmed everywhere. I became aware of having had the
idea for some time that Mirella may have a learning
disability of some type or ADHD. I did not want to pour oil
on the fire and so assessed whether suggesting this would
make things worse between her and Nick. My sense about
Nick was that he would not use this against her. I took the
risk in the next session.

A watershed session. Nick began by saying Mirella's lack
of reliability made him feel that she didn't care about him.
Mirella now seemed more genuinely concerned about this
herself, and we spent some time on her difficulties in finishing
tasks. I then said: "I'm wondering if you have some kind of

learning disability – it's so hard for you to focus on one task at a time and to complete it." Instead of being embarrassed, she stopped defending herself and lit up. "I wonder about that, too. I was tested in high school for a learning disability. I never told Nick. I still have the tests – can I bring them in?" At first Nick laughed, mostly out of embarrassment that this "defect" in his wife was being talked about in such a direct way. He wanted to cover it up, but Mirella did not. Before we ended, he was able to see it as a serious, non-volitional problem.

From here on, the work was, relatively, a breeze. Mirella, now happily exposed, was much more amenable to help. "*M. now seems completely changed – and N. is trying to keep up. Both report things are much better. I asked why. N. said we're more sensitive to each other, there's less yelling. M. said he had rubbed her back when she was anxious and she really appreciated this. She's now noticing her lack of finishing things, and we talked about ADHD. She's developed a system of yellow stickies. N. still putting her down – i.e. 'Now we have stickies all over the house.' When I pointed this out, he was able to say: 'I know. I guess I have a long history of this.' Acknowledged. I was able, for the first time, to notice with him how he uses her lack of organization to get out of doing housework. He said: 'I'm Italian, what do you expect?' Laughter all around. Then he complained again about her whining in the session, which I didn't quite hear as whining. I said it wasn't too bad. He said: 'I have an ear for whining like she has an ear for yelling.'*"

They both came unusually early for the next session – interpreted by me, as I sat in my office, as evidence of how well things were going and how grateful they were to their excellent therapist. I started the session on an upbeat note: "So, things were going much better last time . . . how are you?" Silence. Nick was looking pale, which I hadn't noticed at first. Mirella then spoke very softly, saying that Nick's father, age 74, had just been diagnosed with pancreatic cancer, and they were upset and scared. I reacted in my natural way: "Oh, God. That's terrible. I'm really sorry." Mirella explained how they had found out, directing the attention to herself, protecting

Nick, who was not ready to talk. I went along with this and asked her the questions I would normally have asked Nick. He sat with his head down, fighting back tears. She said they were very caring of their parents, which I knew, and that this was a huge blow for Nick, whom she was very worried about. "I want most of all to take care of my hubby," an unusual term for her to use, which I saw as expressing the closeness she now felt toward him.

I turned to Nick, who said he had nothing to say, and asked him what he knew so far. As he talked, he began sobbing, saying that all he was asking for now was one year, he knew his father was going to die. "I just don't want him to suffer."

By using the example of their therapy, this couple had by now (thankfully) created enough of a holding environment to be able to tolerate this. As we explored Nick's feelings of depression, described by him as filling his body right down to his feet, Mirella sat quietly. He had at first been afraid to leave the house, and then was restless in the house and needed to get out. We talked about what he imagined was going to happen and what he feared most. I was struck by the amount of responsibility he had taken for the whole situation; he was the one the doctor had communicated to – he had to give his father the news, and he saw his role as protecting his father by parcelling out medical information to him. Even though I knew his father did not speak perfect English, the degree of responsibility Nick was carrying seemed excessive. We understood this active role as a coping mechanism.

I asked Nick how his father was dealing with it. "He's depressed and wants to die. He said I should make the funeral arrangements." I said: "I guess that reaction has had a big effect on you." He agreed. Then I asked Mirella how she thought Nick's father was dealing with his diagnosis. "He's OK. I'm close to him and I talked to him about it. He said if there's anything they can do like surgery or chemo, he'll go for it. If not, he wants to go fast. I guess we'd all feel that way." I asked Nick about this discrepancy in perceptions. He shrugged and said that Mirella saw things through rose-coloured glasses. I said: "Mirella seems sad, but you seem depressed." We were then able to talk about how Nick's depression was colouring, to some extent, the way he imagined his father to be feeling. He volunteered that his mother was fine. "She says what will be, will be." Then he smiled and said, "I think she doesn't really care." Again we talked about a possible function of his depression, that is, to prove how much he did care, how much he loved his father. All of this was done in the context of acknowledging how hard a time this was for him and how scared he was.

In terms of their dealing with this crisis *together*, Mirella said, "Sometimes I just sit with him, that's what he wants." I checked that out: had he been able to tell her what he wanted so far and had she been able to provide it? Both agreed, although Mirella was getting anxious about whether she could keep this up. I was extremely impressed with how she had conducted herself during the session – moving in and out at appropriate times, offering gentle comment and helpful information, putting Nick's needs first and doing all the "right" things for him. At the end of the session, she said that she was suffering, too. That had been the trade-off; we all knew it. I told her I understood that, gave her praise for her empathic attunement (not in those words) and said I knew her feelings were getting lost right now. Nick had stopped crying when they left.

In this situation, this couple had been in treatment just long enough to be able to make use of their new skills, built upon their old love for each other, when this crisis occurred. Although I had thought they would need a few more weeks or months of consolidation of the good feelings, they demonstrated they could put them to use immediately; this crisis would constitute the opportunity for consolidation. One could argue that when a therapist sees a couple for as long as I do, the probability of extreme life events or crises arising will be high. This provides the chance to help the couple work their way through a crisis together. The idea is that this experience will generalize to other crises when they are encountered after termination. At the time of writing this, we are in the middle of this crisis and, so far, Mirella and Nick are doing well enough for each other.

Of course, as I have stated earlier, not all partners who come for therapy want to make their relationship work; perhaps it behoves us at this point to look in on a therapy that was directed toward separation.

Linda and Pete, both musicians, who had lived together for thirteen years and had one latency-aged son, had disparate agendas for coming to therapy. Linda, who was the real star musically, was depressed when I first met her. She reported that she was very involved with another female musician who was, at the time of our sessions, dying of cancer. Linda spent most of her free time at the hospital or at this friend's home caring for her. Although she stated they had not had an affair, all of Linda's libidinal energy was obviously tied up with this woman. There was a long history to their relationship. Pete was desperate to keep his relationship with Linda, and declared his love for her at every opportunity in our sessions. Linda would squirm and look at me when this happened, as we both could hear the underlying rage in his voice, which he refused to acknowledge. He stated that even if Linda were in love with this woman, he still wanted to be with her, as the woman was dying anyway!

It became clear over our time together that Linda definitely wanted to separate from Pete, that she no longer loved or respected him, and that she was unsure of her sexuality. She wanted to be on her own. When I said that this was my understanding, her depression began to lift. Pete then became absorbed in enumerating what he considered to be Linda's faults (e.g. messiness at home, inability to care for their son because of her late hours) and talked about their early days when he had looked after her. I suggested he was furious, but he denied it, smiling. It was this smiling rage that evoked paralysing guilt in Linda, because of her experience with a very disturbed mother.

After several months, I asked Linda to state clearly whether she wanted to continue to try in this relationship. At this point, she was able to look directly at Pete and say, "It's over, Pete. I don't want to be with you any more." He began to cry and Linda again looked to me for help.

Our continuing sessions together became focused on trying to understand with Pete why it was so hard for him to let go, including discussing his family history, where he had been responsible for the care of a younger brother who had become violent and addicted to street drugs. One hypothesis was that he may have been trying to take care of Linda in the same way to make up for his perceived failure with his brother; however, although Linda had appeared to be needy, and indeed, sometimes had a little-girl expression on her face, she was a confirmed success in her/their field. I gently advanced the idea that the caretaking position helped him deal with his envy, both of his younger brother (who "got away with murder") and of Linda.

During this time, Pete was finally able to express his anger more directly, as he said he saw no life for himself without Linda. This led us to talk together about their lives after separation – where they would live, how much contact they would have with each other, and, most importantly, how they would manage the parenting of their son. After several of these sessions, in which each partner defensively claimed to be the closest one to their child, Linda reluctantly agreed that Pete should be his main caretaker, provided that she would have access to him when she wanted it. This gave Pete the moral high ground, allowing him both to save face in this humiliating situation and to meet his needs to be a caretaker. He emphasized his triumph by announcing that he had decided to teach music at home, which would certainly confirm that he was the better parent; incidentally, of course, this decision also removed him from further competition with Linda.

Although Linda found it excruciatingly difficult to let go of the major role of parent to their son, her needs for exploring her sexuality and her ambitions in music both contributed to the defensive "logic" of it. They next argued bitterly about how their son should be told the news, as

Linda was feeling intense guilt about her decision. As we rehearsed what each would say to their son, it became evident that Pete could not give the information without angrily blaming Linda. Therefore, it was agreed that Linda should be allowed to tell him first. This was carried out and reported on in a session that was very emotional for all of us, as we moved toward ending. Both individuals said they found the termination phase of the therapy helpful, but Pete acknowledged that he still had his hopes up every time they came for a session. The decision to stop therapy was a painful one for him. They were each offered referrals for individual therapy.

It is difficult to summarize technique by describing only a few cases. However, some of the differences between working with couples and working with individuals have been highlighted in the above examples, including: the possibility of different agendas in starting treatment; the ability to see the relationship *in vivo*; the richness and complication of having another individual contribute to the therapeutic interaction; the need to balance airtime and attention; the unique opportunity to work on an individual issue within the couples context; and the more active involvement of the therapist. The ending phase, which leads to termination, has its own special characteristics in this milieu. Before discussing this phase, it will be helpful to examine in greater detail the issues of transference and countertransference as they are manifested in psychoanalytic couples therapy.

Chapter 5

Transference(s)

As we have seen, psychoanalytically-informed couples therapy has borrowed from and elaborated on many ideas from psychoanalysis and from individual psychoanalytic psychotherapy, including the unconscious and mechanisms of defence. In terms of the concepts of transference and counter-transference, the couples therapist is dealing with multiple, interacting partner-to-therapist and partner-to-partner trans-ferences and countertransferences. In this chapter, the concept of transference will, somewhat artificially, be sifted out from the concept of countertransference for the purpose of high-lighting its special properties in this milieu. The vagaries of the countertransference will be the focus of the next chapter.

> Every beginner in psycho-analysis probably feels alarmed at first at the difficulties in store for him when he comes to interpret the patient's associations and to deal with the reproduction of the repressed. When the time comes, however, he soon learns to look upon these difficulties as insignificant, and instead becomes convinced that the only really serious difficulties he has to meet lie in the manage-ment of the transference.
>
> (Freud, 1915a, p. 159)

The concept of transference has been hailed in psycho-analysis as everything from the greatest obstacle to the treatment to the most important and facilitative aspect of it. In either case, the understanding and analysis of transference phenomena have always been at the very centre of the therapeutic endeavour for psychoanalytic therapists. Different schools of psychoanalysis emphasize different aspects of the definition and the manifestation of transference. Traditionally, the meaning of transference was the displacement of a whole series of positive and negative psychological experiences from the patient's past onto the person of the therapist. Those were the days when the therapist was considered a neutral observer, a blank screen onto which the patient could rather easily project their fantasies, wishes, desires, and fears from past relationships. Earlier, Greenson (1967) said that for a reaction to be considered transference, it must have two characteristics: it must be a repetition of the past and it must be inappropriate to the present. We also know that transference does not only occur in therapeutic situations but is ubiquitous.

The thinking about transference has gone through several iterations since Freud's day, as the concept of a two-person therapy has taken hold. The analyst's role in the creation of the transference, not only their "real" personality characteristics, but their mood, desires, needs – conscious and unconscious – are seen as inevitably part of the result. We repeat Renik's (1993) catchphrase of the "analyst's irreducible subjectivity" as a mantra.

It is not a new assumption that the marital relationship rests, at least in part, on expectations and perceptions that have been transferred from one partner's earlier significant life experiences to the other. To the extent that such "transferences" are gratified or corroborated, the marital relationship may be satisfactory. However, as has been referred to earlier, at least two unsatisfying eventualities can occur: one or more key expectations are sorely disappointed, the partner eventually turning out to be the reverse of what they appeared to be during the courtship; or a life crisis, for example illness, forces a shift in the equilibrium so that the previous "transference" need is no longer gratified.

In couples therapy, because individuals are involved in *reliving* the history of their object relations conflicts and

desires, instead of just reporting it, there is a unique opportunity to understand and make interpretations about the
transference components of the relationship as well as the
transference to the therapist.

> Whereas the individual therapist deliberately conducts
> himself in such a way as to reduce to a minimum the
> limitations of what can be brought into the transference,
> the partners in a marriage are continually defining
> between them the limits of what can be expressed within
> the relationship, such that the "material" that is brought
> to the therapy is, in a sense, pre-defined.
>
> (Colman, 1993, p. 73)

Unresolved oedipal issues, in both the individuals in the
couple are a rich source of conscious and unconscious
transference triggers in this type of therapy. Guttman (1982)
states that when the particular triadic situation of couples
therapy, involving the transference between the partners and
the therapist, is added to the partner transferences, marital
conflicts may be heightened. This allows the therapist to see
them more clearly, make helpful interpretations, and speed
up the process of working through, especially because the
other person is present. The occurrence of the transference-
like process raises the question of identifying the curative
factor in couples therapy, since the traditional resolution of
the transference that indicates a "cure" in individual
psychoanalysis and leads to a more realistic view of the
analyst, is, in a way, already present from the start with
couples.

Being aware of the transferences in working with couples
means thinking about the following permutations and
combinations: the transference of each individual to the
therapist, in other words, how the therapist is represented
for each person; how the therapist is represented for the
couple together; and the transferences of the partners to
each other.

Transferences to the therapist

The *idealizing transference* that is usually present at the start of treatment, as described earlier, is often a nurturing one, as partners need to believe they have found a safe haven at last, and the therapist needs to feel that they think he or she can help them. The idea of expressing negative feelings toward the therapist is too threatening at first, even though a couple may perceive the therapist as withholding, intimidating, or just plain wrong; there are enough negative feelings already in the room. It seems so important to keep the therapist idealized, at least in the beginning and sometimes throughout the treatment, that partners may displace anger and negative feelings onto each other in order to "protect" the therapist. Often this is difficult for a couple to acknowledge, and discussions of why they need to do this may be only minimally productive.

The joint fantasy is that the therapist is in a happy marriage with a wonderfully attuned spouse (whom he or she may have "trained"), and has healthy, normal children who are all successful in their endeavours. Since this is rarely – actually, never – the case, the couples therapist seems even more charged with walking the fine line between real life and the transference expectations of the two partners than is the individual therapist.

To the extent that one sees the real characteristics of the therapist as seeping into the transference, the *gender of the therapist* can be salient (Kalb, 2002). Kulosh and Mayman (1993), who conducted a study on gender-linked determinants in transference and countertransference in individual therapy, found that the therapist's gender is a significant, powerful and organizing influence on the way transferences emerge. Turkel (1992) discusses the *choice* of the therapist by gender. When couples choose a therapist, both partners' fantasies about therapist gender have to coincide, to some extent, and so discussion about this has probably already taken place within the couple in some form (e.g. "Are you OK with seeing a male/female? Will you feel ganged up on/sympathized with?").

"Excuse me for a moment. It's my idiot husband."

The patient's gendered response may trigger a reaction in the therapist. If we think of this as a two-subject co-created influence, then we cannot distinguish absolutely between fantasy and reality. "Instead, transference represents a fluid, perpetually intermingling blend of fantasy and reality, similarity and uniqueness, which focuses on the experiences of both the internal and external relationship. It is inevitably laden with both the . . . [therapist and patient(s)'] reciprocally intertwined gender constructions and actualized by . . . [all] parties" (Kalb, 2002, p. 121). The cartoon at the opening of the next chapter speaks to this issue from the perspective of gender-related countertransference.

At the beginning of treatment, the therapist usually elicits a *parental* transference, and, as therapy progresses, remains in some version of this – expert, teacher, "doctor." As the maternal transference settles onto me, and usually hangs around, in some form, as mentioned above, until the end of treatment, I have found that couples need "parenting" as much or more than individuals. Perhaps it is not particularly surprising that the triadic situation of two patients with one therapist evokes this children–parent dynamic.

Most studies show that in couples therapy, the transferences seem more likely to be congruent with the therapist's gender and other realistic characteristics. I have never had the experience of being the object of a father transference here, as I have occasionally in individual therapy, and more frequently in psychoanalysis. This relates to the limited opportunity for regression in this milieu, as the reminder of reality is ever present in the person of the other partner. Another factor in the dilution of the regressive transference to the therapist in couples therapy may relate to the transfer – or, at least, sharing – of the libidinal action between the therapist and the partner; it also could be a result of the therapist's more active, and hence more "real," involvement with the couple. In fact, the transference seems to lighten as the work goes on.

Couples who come to therapy presenting with their own parenting problems as one of the difficulties in their relationship may see the therapist as the parent they never had, who they hope can provide them with the inner resources to parent their own children. Sometimes a couple in this situation will collusively contrive to bring their young child to the session (e.g. "We couldn't find a babysitter . . ."), so that the therapist can directly observe, help, and indirectly parent them parenting their child. One or two sessions like this, later discussed with the couple, are often very productive for normalizing their anxieties about their child and supporting their parenting skills; as well, and the therapist can see how the couple interact when their child is present. This rich discussion takes place, of course, *after* the babysitter has been re-found.

Complementary to the parental transference is the evoking of the inevitable *sibling* transference in the partners, which yields material rarely seen in individual treatment. The setting is perfect for sibling rivalries. Depending on how the couple relate when they are not in the consulting room – e.g. some couples are already rivalrous in terms of work achievements or household tasks – the couple will respond to the therapist in a more or less competitive manner. The most obvious competition is for the role of the good, wounded person versus the bad, aggressive person. Some couples will go out of their way to fight out these roles for the therapist's "benefit," to vie for the therapist's attention. It is surprising how all ages of partners will resort to tattling on each other, or to scolding each other.

There may also be competition for the limelight, such as it is, or for avoidance of it. In the case of one couple I saw, who had come into therapy to separate, they were often playing "whose session is it anyway." In one session, the female partner referred to the therapy as *his* therapy; he retorted that she felt that way because for once she wasn't taking up the total time.

The wish to have the therapist judge who is "right" is almost always expressed to some extent at the beginning, and with some couples can be prolonged and exaggerated through the treatment (an example of this was mentioned in the report-card behaviour described in the last chapter). These couples may not notice their competition for the therapist, as it is an integral part of how they usually relate, i.e. like siblings.

The therapist's skill in balancing airtime and giving each person attention in turn, as discussed earlier, can limit the sibling rivalry that is aroused from the anxiety of being in this triadic situation. If that is not enough, then tracing the individuals' family experiences, particularly with siblings, will be helpful. When this kind of situation threatens to become destructive to the therapy, it is often found that one or both partners are involved in eternal feuds with a sibling, or do not have any contact with him or her. Analogies may then be helpfully drawn to the relationship of the couple themselves, especially as it manifests itself in the therapy.

Of course, there can be different, or *asymmetrical*, transferences to the therapist in the two partners. In the case of Mirella and Nick, described in the preceding chapter, Mirella developed a dependency on me for some time, which Nick did not *seem* to have. She insisted on saving important discussions for our time together, even though Nick protested that they could surely talk about controversial issues without me. Mirella had found a mother and father in one, and had the natural expectation projected from her past that I would understand and help her. Nick felt that coming for therapy was like taking medicine. It was "OK," but his preference was not to be here. He was impatient with how slowly it moved, whereas Mirella enjoyed the slow, detailed pace. Nick was glad of a recent one-month break, taken because of their holiday, saying that now they would have a chance to try out what they had learned; Mirella appeared sad to have the break.

The therapist must also be aware that the different overt transferences may reflect the couple's internal dynamics. In the case of Mirella and Nick, Mirella knew of Nick's need to be seen as the strong, independent one, and she may have taken the other role to help out. This ensures for Nick that he can keep coming to therapy without having to face his own dependency needs – that is, until this dynamic is explored.

Another window into dissimilar transference reactions is provided when one partner keeps cancelling appointments or one is consistently late. In this situation, the "delinquent" partner evokes a reaction in both the other partner and the therapist, and it is difficult to tell whether one, or both, are the object of the transference fantasy being manifested as a resistance, until it is analysed.

A difference in transference reactions can also come about in the situation where a couple are engaged in the dichotomy of caretaker–cared-for, mentioned in the last chapter. The cared-for partner may make a switch to the therapist as caretaker, while the caretaker partner feels threatened and competes with the therapist. In the case of Gail and John, the couple who met when Gail was a graduate student in John's department, introduced briefly in Chapter 3, Gail, fifteen years younger than John, was often in the position of being looked after. At first, John did not seem to mind that I was taking over in this role with her; in fact, it sometimes seemed that he appreciated it. There came a time, however, when he needed to be part of the interaction, especially when Gail was complaining about issues other than their marriage. At these times, John (who was very close to my age) and I became parents together. I particularly remember that at the time of 9/11, Gail was extremely anxious, afraid to travel in the city, certain that Toronto would soon be under attack. John and I were both involved in trying to help her feel calmer, which she actually seemed to like very much. In fact, *both* were smiling as I communicated that observation, confirming my dawning sense that I was participating in an enactment, as McLaughlin (1991) defined it. John's gratification at our mutual participation may have been: *You can see what I have to deal with; or, I'm as good or better at helping her than you; or you and I are one.*

The fantasy of being identified with the parent (in my case, mother) in playing co-therapist is a special type of transference in couples therapy, as there is a "child" in opposition to whom one stands. This idea is also evident in the report-card behaviour, and was seen in the example of Lisa and Eric who were working on issues of separation from Lisa's parents. A scientific enquiry into the different transferences of each (opposite- or same-sex) partner to the one therapist, and their effects on outcome, would be interesting, but is beyond the scope of this book.

There are some couples who strongly want to be admired *as a couple* (Sharpe, in Solomon and Siegel, 1997), over-shadowing in the beginning their individual competition for the therapist's approval. This is known as the *whole couple transference.* This type of couple often present as playful in exhibiting their wit and charm, and may even be entertaining. I once saw a couple who started each session with comedy routines, as if they were on stage. They were very amusing, at first, with jokes that were sometimes spontaneous, and that sometimes seemed already practised in social situations. These types of couples strive to be the therapist's favourite couple, and often succeed – at least for a while. Their joint idealizing transference to the therapist often evokes a corresponding idealization of the couple.

The good news about borderline couples who are locked in chronic dysharmony and who have an angry and negative whole couple transference to the therapist (as happened in the case of Rita and Stan, described briefly in Chapter 2) is that at least they can unite about something. Both Rita and Stan had a historical tendency to use denial and splitting as defences. Making me into the inadequate and incompetent one served the function of a mutual denial and splitting off of undesirable traits in themselves and in each other, to some extent. They then were able to react negatively or punitively to me, which seemed, miraculously, to make their marriage better – at least in the first month or two. In fact, when they left our sessions after fighting loudly with each other, and telling me that I didn't understand them at all, they always remarked that they felt much better, and their week together went well. (*Glad to be of service*, I would say to myself.)

There may, of course, be a private "whole couple" transference that is difficult to discern – i.e. how the couple talk about the therapist when they are not with him or her. Sometimes how they refer to me when they are alone together slips out – for example, one couple, in describing a conversation they had, unwittingly referred to me as "the Ush." I was unsure what to make of this; somewhat embarrassed, they quickly assured me it was a term of affection.

Individual *erotic transferences* seem much more diluted, if they occur at all. It is hard to flirt with someone with your partner present. The way I have sometimes noticed them is in the discomfort that (mostly) male partners may feel when they are left alone with me. In the way I work, this does not happen when they arrive early, as I ask them to wait in the waiting room until their partner arrives; it only occurs if their partner leaves the session momentarily to use the washroom or take a cellphone call. However, the resultant discomfort may partly be accounted for by the therapy set-up, which is that we are always a threesome, so that a twosome feels unusual. If I think erotic feelings are present unconsciously, I hesitate to interpret them unless they are getting in the way.

A whole couple unconscious erotic transference, however, may be a different story. When the therapist is seen in a couple's life as someone to whom they can talk openly about sex for the first time, the therapist's being incorporated, or included somehow, in their sexual life is a distinct possibility. I have seen this manifested in varying degrees: from a couple arguing in bed together saying "What do you think Dr Usher would say about this?" to a couple (Anne and Michael) who haven't had sex for a long time telling me (jokingly?) that they'll leave me a voicemail message when they do. One sexually troubled couple who were trying to stimulate their intimate life developed the idea – one weekend during their therapy – of having a threesome in bed, and actually crafted an ad for the local newspaper. Since they brought it to the session first for discussion, I was able to interpret the fantasy of having me in bed with them – which both agreed they would like! Now, an overly zealous reader might comment on the countertransference contribution to this fantasy: was I turned on by one, or both, of them? Had I had (unconscious, of course) fantasies of threesomes? Or did I just need to be included so badly in this oedipal couple that I'd go for anything? Chapter 6, on countertransference, answers these and other perplexing questions a couples therapist must ask him- or herself.

(A note here on the above couple referring to me as "Dr Usher." I do not indicate a preference as to how any of the people I see should refer to me, but leave that as a bit of grist for the transference mill. Interestingly, there always appears to be consistency *within* the couple. Professionals of about my age may refer to me on a first-name basis, although this occurs overall less frequently with couples than in individual therapy, as the parental transference is a sticky one. Older or younger couples usually prefer "Dr," as do couples who are working towards separation.)

I have never been the object of a *sibling transference*, i.e. older brother or sister, in couples therapy, as I have in individual therapy. This could be because the sibling is already present in the room, or because, as noted above, people seem to need an "authority" type of person when their intimate relationship is threatened.

Partner-to-partner transferences

In Chapter 3 there was a discussion of object choice, which gave some idea of the transferences and projections manifested within a relationship. Has the individual paired off with mother, father, sibling, or a combination? Have the transferences changed since the relationship began, and if so how and why?

> What each marital partner brings to a marriage is an internal psychic model that comprises childhood events and fantasies about his or her own parents and their relationship. These internal parents are never wholly realistic because they are always filtered through a multitude of complex unconscious feelings such as idealization, envy, sexual longings and rivalries . . . hostility and dependent yearnings.
>
> (Frank, 1997, p. 87)

Thus there are many opportunities for within-couple transferences, as has been noted, depending on the perceptions of the parents' marriages and their derived expectations about how they themselves will be treated by a committed partner. It will also depend on the developmental milestones achieved – particularly the resolution of oedipal conflicts and separation-individuation issues.

The possible sibling transferences within the partnership, both in relation to the therapist and in relation to each other, have been described earlier.

"This is my wife—the founder and executive director of our marriage."

Some writers have found it helpful to organize couples into types to predict possible partner-to-partner transferences. Sharpe (1997), for example, describes the differences in reactions in what she refers to as the "oppositional" couple – whose interaction is dominated by dependence–independence conflicts, as distinguished from the "symbiotic" couple. Partners in the oppositional couple are always opposing what the other partner wants or values, either in open combat or covert resistance. This, of course, interferes successfully with emotional intimacy. Sharpe's description of the symbiotic couple, on the other hand, is of two people with a merged, blurred boundary between them, which often successfully interferes with sexual intimacy. Both these types of couples have had difficulty in the separation-individuation phase. Oppositional couples may share the internal objects of a critical and controlling parent; symbiotic couples may have had parents who did not support individuation but rewarded compliance. Both couples may be locked in a struggle for validation from the other, and for permission to be independent without fear of abandonment or destruction of the relationship. In these situations, the spouse represents the disapproving or needful parent, and the partner acts accordingly.

The idea of partner-to-partner transferences fits the conceptualizations of the intersubjectivists who state that whatever takes place between the two partners is determined by mutual influence, and that psychopathology should not be considered apart from the context in which it is expressed. Speaking to the unconscious level on which the partners relate, this perspective raises the possibility that what on the surface may look like unequal levels of disturbance in a relationship, may, on a deeper level, turn out to be dyadically co-constructed (Berkowitz, 1999).

Within-couple transferences are often appropriate to the environment; therefore, to understand the transference, we must understand the individual's experience of the current here-and-now climate that has contributed to it. When one member of a couple acts in accordance with the other's transference expectations because it taps into a defensive way of acting that was adaptive for them in earlier days, the partner-to-partner transference becomes credible, or plausible. This interaction in the couple is reciprocally influential, like the interplay of transference and countertransference in therapy with individuals. In the earlier example, when Gail began to depend on me instead of John for caretaking, John felt he didn't matter and was no longer needed, and so found a way of joining me in helping Gail. Being needed and helpful had been the only way he had been able to gain self-esteem in an emotionally impoverished childhood household. When Mirella demanded more affection from Nick, he bristled, because his earlier experience with a needy mother had made him feel controlled and intruded upon. Although bristling and moving away might have been adaptive in the situation with his mother, we saw how it was not adaptive with Mirella.

Kohut's (1977) concept of selfobject transferences is relevant here. The mirroring, idealizing, and, particularly, twin-ship selfobject functions speak not only to the experience of falling in love, but also to the feeling of being alike, that many partners maintain. (Just as people begin to look like their pets after some years, they may also start to resemble their partners.) One partner's narcissistic need to make the other fit their perception of a perfect match – as in, *When we look in the mirror, we are a great couple!* – is a special kind of partner-to-partner selfobject transference.

Interpreting the between-partners transferences has always seemed to me more urgent, more useful – and more interesting – than interpreting each individual's, or even the whole couple's, transference to me. The relationship with the therapist here seems less important than in individual therapy; I actually spend considerable time in the background as the therapy goes on. This does not mean that there are not times when there are virulent transferences to me, as we have seen earlier, but this occurs much less frequently with couples. And I do not attempt to stir them up. I try to maintain the position of a benign, positive, caring helper, whose focus is on the relationship between the two partners.

As therapy progresses, and these partner-to-partner transferences are explored and (co-)interpreted, individuals begin to understand how these deep connections may be affecting the relationship in a negative (or positive) way. Then it is easier to cooperate in working towards change. When this happens, the internal shifts in each are noticed and remarked on by both partners, as they manifest themselves in overt behaviours. The shifts in the interactions of the couple are similarly noticed and are very clearly self-reinforcing.

Chapter 6

Countertransference

"Look, there is no right and wrong here, but I'm going
to side with Helen because I'm a girl."

Countertransference is composed of the therapist's personal
or subjective reactions to the patient, and is usually thought to
include all of his or her responses, conscious and unconscious
– with particular attention being paid to those responses that
constitute a departure from the therapist's typical therapeutic
style. As is now well known, these reactions were originally
regarded as an impediment to psychoanalytic treatment.
Freud did not doubt that countertransference was an
"insidious obstruction to the analyst's benevolent neutrality,
a resistance to be diagnosed and defeated" (Gay, 1988, p. 254).

Gay cites Freud's 1910 paper on the future prospects of psychoanalysis: "The analyst must recognize this counter-transference in himself and master it . . . every psychoanalyst only gets as far as his own complexes and inner resistances allow" (p. 254). Perhaps the admonishment was meant for Freud himself and his dearest colleagues, for what Freud learned very early on from his own work with Dora and from Breuer's experience with Anna O. was that therapists could be hurt, they could be made angry, and they could be tempted to respond to seductive behaviour, and that these emotions seriously clouded a therapist's perceptions. Still, the awareness of countertransference seemed to come as such a surprise that it is no wonder Freud tried to shake it off at first, advising his colleagues and students to have more analysis to get rid of it.

Just after Freud's time, it was thought that we should give countertransference more attention and more study, if only because it was seen to be stirred up by the patient. Theorists agreed that some of the feelings evoked in the therapist had been projected into or onto him or her by the patient – in the case of couples, we would say by both patients – for defensive, evacuative purposes and also as a means of communicating a person's internal world. The task of the therapist was then to become consciously aware of what feelings and fantasies were being aroused, to make some sense of them, and to offer some understanding to the patient(s) through an interpretation or comment (Ruszczynski, 1993), or possibly even an enactment – hopefully to be analysed.

Later, the relationalist ideas about the therapist's subjectivity added another dimension to our understanding of countertransference phenomena. The concept of counter-transference was broadened to include the therapist's contribution, in response to the patient's transference, to the patient as an individual, and to the material brought into the sessions that related to specific unresolved issues in the therapist. The many ways in which the patient gratified or frustrated the therapist were also seen as evoking counter-transference reactions. Now hailed as "the news from within," it is seen as a most important source of information for the therapist, and in some limited cases, for the patient, on many levels of the therapy.

Siegel (Solomon and Siegel, 1997) talks about the selective factor in choosing psychotherapy as a career, suggesting that as therapists we bring a certain commonality to the counter-transference: "a need to relate more intimately to others, to understand oneself better, to repeat a pattern of caretaking that began in childhood, to resolve personal problems, or to meet needs for power, admiration and love" (p. 6).

Although there has not been a great deal of research in the area of countertransference in couples work, what has been written so far is extremely thoughtful (see, for example, Solomon and Siegel, 1997). Being in a triangular situation is usually our first experience of family life, yet it is often one of the most difficult to manage successfully. Triads too often become coalitions of two against one, or fusions of two or three members into pseudomutuality, or even collusive distancing (Guttman, 1982).

In working with couples, opportunities to meet one's caretaking needs are omnipresent. Voyeuristic urges, even though consciously denied, can be gratified almost too easily as the therapist peers into the intimate workings of the couple's relationship. In addition, Frank (1997) states, and I agree, that too often couples therapists fail to explore oedipal issues, focusing instead on narcissistic injury and rage, fears of abandonment, and on exposing pathological projective identification. Frank feels that this avoidance is due to oedipal countertransference anxiety – in other words, a fear of dealing with one's own oedipal conflicts. He gives as an example a young therapist who may shy away from openly discussing the couple's sexual life because of his childhood prohibitions against sexual curiosity about parental intercourse. There is also the risk of repetition of a childhood need to repair a parental marriage that is perceived as bad, whether depressed or violent. We sometimes can notice this when we begin to offer suggestions to the couple, rules to live by. Same-sex rivalry, where the therapist unconsciously competes with same-sex partner to show the other-sex partner that they are the better, more understanding spouse, is also an indication of oedipal countertransference.

The current relationship life of the therapist – whether he or she is in an intimate relationship, wants to be or doesn't want to be; whether their relationship is relatively smooth or highly stressful; or whether they are recently divorced – will affect their work with couples.

Since the couple's impossible, idealizing expectations, referred to in the last chapter, may include the therapist fixing a marriage *and* fixing two individuals, the opportunities for arousing grandiose and saviour fantasies in the countertransference are many.

Every facet of the couple's therapist's work creates the risk for overidentification, envy, feelings of exclusion and grandiosity, and even regression, in facing two people who are intensely involved in a troubled relationship, and wanting a their help. Countertransferences in couples therapy are often more frequent and compelling than those of the individual therapist, and are usually more complex, as the therapist has to be aware of his or her reactions towards more than one patient at the same time.

> I have found that countertransference reactions engendered in couples therapy are more potent, complex, chaotic, and unruly than those activated in individual treatment . . . . Being in the middle of a ferocious fight provokes far more intense reactions than hearing about the fight in individual therapy.
>
> (Sharpe, 1997, p. 40)

Monitoring countertransference responses can be complicated, but is very necessary if the therapist is to keep afloat in a sea of continuous waves: am I identifying with the struggles of both partners and entering into each of their inner worlds? Or am I feeling more of an affiliation with one and seeing their perception of the "bad" other as accurate? Do I admire/idealize one partner or both? Does one partner remind me of a parent or sibling? Is this relationship better than mine? Am

I sexually attracted to either partner? Am I overly curious or not curious enough about their intimate life together? Am I worried about what they think about me? Do I prepare for their sessions differently from usual? Do I regret, or am I particularly proud of, my participation after they have left? Considering that a countertransference-based interpretation is the most potent therapeutic tool we have, should any of these feelings or fantasies be deliberately disclosed to the couple? The answer to this last question is: rarely, but probably more often than in individual therapy.

If therapists remain unaware of their reactions to a couple, their inappropriate responses can include being chronically late for sessions, constantly putting the same spouse (often the rival) on the spot, ignoring the couple's blatantly provocative statements or behaviour (Guttman, 1982) or even finding a way of prematurely terminating the case. Like transferences, countertransferences are fluid and can change and shift at different stages of the therapy.

Often, therapists find themselves forced into either a parental or a child role with respect to the couple. We have seen earlier that the therapist as parent/teacher to the two "kids" is a common dynamic in this therapeutic triad. For some therapists, this can be a gratifying role as it enables one to be the loving and wise parent to squabbling siblings in, sometimes, a more effective manner than one has been able to accomplish in one's own life. The feeling of being competed for is also gratifying for some therapists; others, however, may find this intimidating. Younger therapists may find it difficult to be parentified, particularly with a couple who are older, and this evokes for them, as it does for all of us in some way, unsettled oedipal issues.

The therapist as child, looking in on the oedipal couple, often triggers a powerful form of countertransference. Feeling excluded from the couple's marital bed and their private space, the therapist may use the voyeuristic aspects of the therapy as a way of gaining admittance into the relationship, or may need to have themselves included by becoming indispensable to the couple. Frank (1997), mentioned earlier, openly describes a case where he saw a couple in treatment as more unhappy than they actually were, and interprets his perception as a defence against his anxiety about being excluded from their intimacy, protecting himself from jealousy and envy.

In the role of child, the therapist may have a tendency to see all the pathology in one partner, corresponding to his or her view of different-sex parents. In addition, the experience of being a helpless child with fighting parents can arouse feelings of being overwhelmed and powerless when treating an argumentative couple; having the opportunity to repair the parental marriage, now seen through the eyes of a professional adult, can be so appealing that therapeutic zeal may actually get in the way, particularly if it is better for a couple to separate.

Envy, often seen as insidious and destructive, may be particularly virulent in the countertransference when treating couples, again because of the link to the oedipal couple. Even though we know that many of the emotions connected with idealization, avoidance, devaluation, and contempt are rooted in envy, envy of patients is considered almost shameful. Therefore, there is not much in the literature about the arousal of envy in the countertransference. The unconscious nature of most envious feelings may also account for the paucity of writing.

In work with couples, there may be much to envy. Feelings like "I wish I could have what he's giving her," or "I would be nicer to him than that," can easily be stirred up as we watch couples interact (West and Schain-West, 1997). West and Schain-West also enumerate many patient qualities of which a therapist can be envious, including youth, beauty, wealth, children, ability to love and be loved, ability to be carefree, or even to stand up for him- or herself. As a non-medical practitioner working in a province in Canada where the fees of medical practitioners are completely covered by government insurance, I am often in the position of seeing only those patients who can afford to pay a private fee for long-term treatment; these couples are often financially better off than I am. Therefore, when I hear arguments about whose turn it is to remove the swimming-pool cover, for example, I may feel a twinge or two. I am also aware, perhaps in a rush of grandiose delusion, of being envious of the couple for having me – an attuned, reliably available therapist, who is interested in them and their problems and wants very much to help their relationship be more satisfying. Their entitlement to this is something I might not indulge for myself.

Of course, like all countertransference feelings, feelings of envy can be obstructive or productive. Envy of a couple's sexual activity, for example, can blind a therapist to underlying issues, such as their using sex as a defence against intimacy and closeness. Empathic listening may be impaired, as may the validation of a partner's ideas or interventions in the therapeutic process – especially if they sound better than the therapist's. Mingling of unconscious envy with a conscious desire to be helpful can lead the therapist to feel confused or ambivalent about the treatment. A therapist's need to be needed by the couple, and then feeling sad and left out when no longer needed, may lead to an envious sabotage of the couple's progress together. As West and Schain-West (1997) have said, couples as patients can often kindle awareness of our own missed or misused opportunities in life, as well as opportunities that we will never have.

Following are examples of countertransference with couples.

"Positive" countertransference

Anne and Michael, the lawyers who work together, have been introduced to the reader earlier in Chapter 1. I described there how I had acted as a container for Michael's anger – their presenting problem – in the sessions, thus attempting to detoxify it for both him and Anne. They had been referred to me by Anne's family doctor, after she had burst into tears about their marriage during a physical examination.

I am going to select one part of their treatment because it touched me so deeply that I felt at once sad, grateful, guilty, and overly competent.

About six weeks into our work together, Michael disclosed that he had been diagnosed with hepatitis C about one year ago. It had apparently gone undetected for twenty-five years, having been acquired through contact with a dirty needle during a one-time use of injectable drugs in his early twenties. When we first discussed it in the session, in addition to reporting their shock at the diagnosis, they both described a subsequent event that had been traumatic for them. This event had occurred as a result of a liver biopsy, part of the diagnostic procedure, which had gone wrong, unknown to them. A few days after this procedure, they had taken their son to Rome for the school break. On the second night there, Michael had become violently ill and had to be admitted to hospital, where he had surgery and remained, close to death, for about one month. Of course there were many repercussions to this critical incident, but one that they now needed to discuss was Anne's inability to comfort Michael during that time, as he was delusional and very angry. He was finally transferred back to hospital in Toronto and recovered slowly. The telling of this event and the resultant guarded prognosis for Michael's illness paralleled a critical incident in my life.

This couple came to see me exactly two months after the death of my own analyst, who died while I was still in analysis. He had been suddenly diagnosed with stage IV cancer, with both bone and brain metastases. He had informed me of the illness and its prognosis as soon as he knew about it. I then had colluded with him in not discussing it any further, despite noticing marked decay in his physical appearance as time went on, as well as a personality change, probably attributable to the brain involvement. The denial suited us both, at least in the beginning. His illness progressed rapidly: three months after the diagnosis, I received a telephone call from him saying that he had been advised to close his practice. We met for one last horrible time.

During the remaining time until his death two months later, he (and his wife) did not want any contact with analysands – no phone calls, cards, or email. Thus, information on his condition was hard to come by, except for the odd bits garnered from colleagues, all of whom were so excruciatingly aware of possible transference issues that they avoided saying much – or even giving support. Galatzer-Levy (2004) has written an excellent article on this subject.

Therefore, when Michael began talking about his fear of dying from hepatitis C, I was, admittedly, countertransferentially challenged. Here was an opportunity to be an integral part of a couple's process regarding serious illness and possible dying, to be informed about their feelings every step of the way, and – maybe – to be of help to them, a role I was prevented from having in my own situation with my analyst. The subject was naturally very hard for both of them to discuss, especially in the light of their serious marital difficulties which had caused them to consider separation, and which were, of course, complicated by this relatively recent diagnosis. They had talked to no one about it: ageing parents were considered too vulnerable, and friends were hard to trust as they feared that if the word got out, they would lose their clients and the firm would collapse. They had not been able to communicate with each other about it since the Rome fiasco.

During the early months of our time together, whenever this subject came up, which varied in frequency, Anne cried and Michael became angry, partly in response to her tears. We spent many sessions on the month of illness in Italy, where Anne said Michael severely rejected her after the surgery. Michael had no memory of this, but apparently had behaved so badly that it was hard for her to forgive. I spent some time with Anne on her resentment at having a sick husband, which was not allowed to be acknowledged because of Michael's potential rage and also because, in quieter moments, Michael admitted that he felt guilty for bringing this on his family and himself. During these early times, I tried to get across to them the traumatic effect of the illness, saying it had been too much to handle. This seemed like news to them at first; later, they began referring to it as "the trauma."

Anne then brought in a dream:

I was on a bus carrying a large turtle. It had a soft shell with a big hole down it as if someone stepped on it with high heels. I was responsible for taking care of it. It was squirming around in my lap. I was having trouble.

Anne quickly declared that she had no associations to the dream. Michael said: "The turtle is me. But you're not responsible for me – don't worry." My understanding of this combination of the dream and the lack of associations to it was that Anne was still very uncomfortable communicating directly anything about Michael's illness that might be construed as negative. Our discussion about this led to Michael's increasing ability to see the effect of his illness and his attitude about it on her.

In one session, Anne complained that when Michael had first learned of his diagnosis, he told her in the hospital parking lot that he had "six years to live." She found this aggressive and hurtful. I asked if he had wanted to hurt her; he wasn't sure. I said that when people think they are dying, they may feel angry at or envious of others who are healthy, and who have no idea what it's like to be in their situation. Both of them looked at me with rapt attention. Michael agreed; then, trying to be empathic and to soften his anger, said: "Of course it'll be hard for Anne when I die because I'm not there and she has to deal with the firm and our son." I said, somewhat mockingly, "Yah. It's easy for *you*." He laughed hard, as did Anne through her tears.

As the sessions went on, and they described in detail their anxieties, my need to be included in this horrendous process with a couple was getting so easily met, I hardly noticed it. After several months of our work together, Michael was scheduled to have a blood test which would indicate whether two years of a chemical drug treatment had had an effect on the hepatitis C. Before he was to meet with the doctor, Anne, who was going along to the appointment, came to the session with a pad and pen, asking if we could formulate what questions to ask. Her contention was that Michael was too cavalier with the doctors and didn't press them enough; he described her as "lobbing grenades" at them. We worked through questions that were comfortable for both. I must have looked very concerned at this point, because Michael, uncharacteristically, leaned over toward me and said: "Don't worry. It's going to be all right." (*Great*, I thought, *now I've got him, in the analyst-transference, looking after me*.)

The news from the doctor was mixed; liver function was stable, but the virus was still there. In terms of the six years pronouncement, they now were not sure; cures might well be discovered sooner than that and since Michael felt relatively well, he might be expected to live much longer. Anne started to feel panicky again, and asked me what people do in this situation. (*I wish I knew*, I thought.) I advised them to put as much of the practical stuff in order as they could, and then to live their lives. They talked about their wills, the firm, and their son. I was by now startlingly aware of my interest in being part of the real nuts and bolts of this process.

In the next session, Michael brought in a work problem which we discussed energetically. Then, Anne started the following session by saying she felt guilty about that previous session. I interpreted to them that we had *all* engaged in a flight, to get some relief from the business of sickness and possible dying. Subsequently, Michael became much less angry and was more able to talk directly to Anne, to reassure her that he felt better and that he wanted to take better care of himself physically.

There was still a lot of emotion in our sessions, and they still fought about their business problems. Also, Michael's anger, at least that part of it that was not directly related to the illness, although less and less frequent, was still erupting on occasion and remained an issue for Anne. In one session, Anne, in her sensible way, made the following statements, which Michael and I, impressed, immediately acceded to. She said she wanted to map out what they had been through in the last nine months – his chemo treatment, the prognosis, and the business and marriage problems, and think now about starting a "new landscape." "Michael has a chronic illness, and needs to take care of his general health," she said.

"We are overly busy at work and need to spend more family time. We need to move forward on this new landscape. Something may happen where we'll step off the landscape, but then we can get back on."

That spring there was an opportunity for a family trip to Rome, and Michael seized it. In the session after they returned, he described going back to the hospital where he had almost died exactly two years before. He visited the ward and his room – "someone else was in it." He said he didn't feel sad, he felt it was really over. He had planned to sit and read a book on the same bench in the hospital garden where he used to sit, but some nurses were practising for a fire drill and he couldn't concentrate. None of the doctors and nurses that he had known were there. "They had probably been promoted," he said, indirectly showing his gratitude.

"Talk about working through," I wrote in my notes. *"I am constantly impressed by how quickly and deeply both of them get this – particularly M. who started out so defensive and angry. I feel we are doing such good work, particularly – maybe only? – around the whole possible death issue. I hope I'll now be able to let them move on to other issues."*

"Negative" countertransference

Unfortunately, as we would expect, the countertransference is not all roses and loving parenting, despite the therapist's conscious need to be all things to all people. I have been in situations where I have had a negative countertransference response to one or both partners in the couple, and have found myself wishing that the therapy would not "work," i.e. that the couple would break up!

In one situation, Lara, the young wife, was, for want of a better descriptor, a gold-digger. Allan, the financially successful husband, had been in one failed marriage, and very much wanted this marriage to work. They lived in a beautiful home and had a full-time nanny for their 8-year-old daughter, despite the fact that Lara was at home. In their courtship, Lara had portrayed herself as an indigent waif, needing rescuing, which captured Allan's imagination, as well as his character pathology. Now she came to therapy complaining that he wouldn't give her enough money. Catching the glare of her diamond ring, which must have been at least 2 carats (see the section on "countertransference envy"), and being oppressed by her appearance in sessions so inappropriately over-dressed, I began to feel like the poor maid-servant. "Why doesn't he see it?" I kept asking myself about Allan. "He's aggressive at the office, but he lets her walk all over him at home."

As the therapy went on, and Allan began reporting rather compliantly that things were much better between them, I may have winced noticeably. Lara, who stated that she really wanted the marriage to last (although she had seen a lawyer regarding her financial rights), began trying to enlist my favour by making female-to-female comments – for example, "Can you believe he gave his ex-wife a key to our house?" – and when I raised an eyebrow, said to Allan, "See, all women react the same way I do." Since I really don't like the game of *gotcha*, especially when I am the one gotten, this heightened my negative response to her, which, by now, I had stopped trying to connect to my past (when my family had less money than many of my friends' families). I tried instead to determine what Allan wanted, and why he could not articulate what he wanted to Lara, relating it to his early relationship with a critical and domineering father, whom he could never please. In this couple, Allan seemed to be the partner most interested in understanding what had happened to make this relationship stop working; Lara *seemed* to be learning by listening and observing. Since they both wanted the relationship to work (and I was the one with the discrepant agenda), we worked at negotiating what they needed from each other in a fairly unemotional manner that made sense to both of them.

In another situation, the couple had been ordered by the court to come for therapy after the husband, Leo, an office manager, had beaten his wife, Fiona, a physician, so badly that she went to the Emergency Room of a nearby hospital where they encouraged her to press charges. As a result, he was forced to live separately from her until his trial, which was about one year away. Issues of bullying get to me. My countertransference response began with the initial telephone call, and I considered referring them to someone else; still, the challenge of taking on a bully from a position of relative power, and maybe even precipitating some change, was one I could not bring myself to turn down.

Leo was all I had imagined him to be, and much more. He showed little remorse for his actions and, in fact, blamed Fiona for provoking him by not answering her cellphone when he called. This was not the first time he had hit her, but it was the worst time. Leo described their fight over the cellphone as though he had been the wronged one. Added to this was his indignation over the ensuing enforced isolation from her, more rent to pay for a separate apartment, a bleeding ulcer that had erupted "because of her," and the possibility of a jail term that would wreck both their lives. It was difficult to get a rapport with these two, and indeed, if they hadn't been in therapy at gunpoint, so to speak, I probably would not have managed it.

Leo and Fiona were both of Middle Eastern background, and had many friends and cultural interests in common. Leo, who was ten years older than Fiona, was the acknowledged expert on music, art, home decorating, in fact, all dimensions of their lives together. When they started therapy, Fiona was certain that the whole episode of the cellphone was her fault and that she should not have reported him; she cringed in submission whenever Leo spoke. The tyrant–supplicant dynamic was a tough one to ease off. Fiona had been in this type of relationship with an intruding and over-controlling mother, who told her what to do in every aspect of her life and she had obeyed – except her mother did not approve of Leo. Leo easily took over the mother's role, and fought so much with Fiona's mother, that it was agreed (by both Leo and Fiona) that her mother was not allowed in their house, and was not even allowed to telephone on their home phone; hence the acquisition of a cellphone.

Interpretations of the dynamics between them revolved around Leo's contempt for his own felt "weakness" and masochistic tendencies which he had projected onto Fiona, and Fiona's need to maintain the status quo – all of these observations were, of course, delivered very cautiously and slowly. My comments were usually met with interest by Fiona and bored resistance by Leo. Balancing airtime was difficult at first, but when, in one session, they brought me a cartoon of two kids fighting and then fought like two kids over who would get to show the cartoon to me, I began to realize how much each of them needed care in terms of their individual concerns: for Leo, it was his health; for Fiona, it was her being overworked.

After these concerns were identified, things went a little better and they began to trust me more, and described in detail fights over shopping, cooking, and many other facets of their lives. In all of them, Leo would become extremely impatient with Fiona, and either mock her or yell. There were many times when, to gratify my own countertransference needs, I directed statements to Leo on Fiona's behalf, indicating that his behaviour was inappropriate, and role modelling some arguing strategies with him. I found myself saying things to him that I knew Fiona could not say. When this happened, Fiona could hardly keep from applauding which, of course, I was keenly aware of. "Finally things are getting said!" she declared. Leo seemed to have met his match, and was even able to start to think of himself as a "bully." Fiona was amazed that someone could engage Leo in this manner (albeit in confined circumstances) and became emboldened herself. She began to yell back at him, and then would look at me and laugh like a scared child – as if to say, "Is this really OK?" Getting her to talk rather than yell was not too hard from there. When they both realized that this was a way to gain approval, even Leo seemed to be learning something, and they took to arguing with each other with me observing, watching for my reaction; they then were able to negotiate more effectively at home and report back to me about it.

Here was an example where my overidentification in the countertransference was made somewhat useful by emboldening a patient in the way I wished I could have been emboldened in my own early life. It also confirmed for me a disidentification with bullies, as well as a taming of them. This couple stayed in treatment past their mandated time. One of the outcomes of their therapy was that Fiona developed a close friendship with another woman, and really enjoyed her company – shopping, going to movies, having coffee out. She had not had a close friend before. I saw this as an externalization of the transference, made possible because she had finally felt validated.

Using the countertransference

The therapist's ability to conceive of a triangular relationship, rather than a dyadic one – in other words, the therapist's own stage of developmental achievement – will contribute to the ease with which they will be able to work with couples. As can be seen, therapy with couples evokes intense countertransference feelings and fantasies. The pre-oedipal needs of some couples to have an all-giving, all-nurturing mother with whom to merge, as they try to do with each other, can evoke feelings of bliss in the therapist, or feelings of intrusion and annoyance. As we have seen, the oedipal countertransference constitutes a reactivation of the therapist's own oedipal experience and unresolved longings.

> In reexperiencing the oedipal child's central conflict, the therapist typically shifts back and forth from idealizing the couple as a parental unit (in the wish to sustain both partners' love) to the oedipal idealization of one partner (including the wish to win that partner away from the other). It is the positive oedipal constellation that is most strongly evoked.
>
> (Sharpe, 1997, p. 65)

Although an absolutely even-handed empathic approach is extremely difficult – and trying to effect a blank screen in couples therapy seems impossible – most couples therapists work hard at balancing airtime, and at making a conscious effort to avoid identification with, or wooing of, one partner. In my experience, as was noted earlier, countertransferences and identifications are fluid during the process of the therapy, if one is open to noticing this. As the therapist gets to know each individual more deeply, it is usually difficult to maintain a desirable–undesirable split in the partners in the counter-transference.

Boundary setting is more difficult, and just as important, in couples therapy as in individual therapy. The therapist's good nature is imposed upon by two people asking for special consideration, including telephone calls and individual meetings. Some of this behaviour is predictable, and interpretable, from the patients' histories; some, when presented urgently from an admired patient and not predicted, appeals to the therapist's grandiosity and unconscious need for an oedipal victory, and may be hard to turn down.

As McLaughlin (1991) said, there are always plenty of "dumb spots, blind spots, and hard spots" to be navigated for the individual therapist. The couples therapist's behaviour and personality seem more in evidence, and therefore their countertransference reactions are more transparent, than those of the individual therapist. There are many subtle communications of our countertransference – in the way we listen, whom we face more often, whom we address or smile at more frequently, our expressions of interest or lack thereof – that are conveyed every moment and usually picked up, consciously or unconsciously, by one or both partners. Acknowledgement of these reactions is always helpful. The therapist can then analyse, privately, whether these observations feel "accurate," and whether they indicate a dynamic between the partners or between the partners and the therapist that would be worth commenting on.

As has been mentioned earlier, the therapeutic triad is ripe for projective identifications, probably in all directions. Being provoked to accept feelings and roles that pertain directly to the partners' internal object relations can be a source of countertransference confusion and anxiety. However, it is also an amazing source of information: as therapists struggle with their own internal responses, they become aware of getting a sense of each individual's dynamics and of what the couple do to each other. Sandler's (1976) concept of the therapist's free-floating responsiveness is a necessary, though difficult, condition for this type of work.

In many ways, making use of the countertransference with a couple may be easier than it is in individual therapy. Although a lot has been said about the opportunities for power in the therapist, there is also the chance that the therapist's pearls of wisdom may be significantly diluted by the couple, either because of sheer numbers, or because partners can react against them or dismiss them outside of the session when they are alone together. Because of this, and because there is always a witness to what I say, I communicate my countertransference reactions more frequently (sometimes) with couples than I do with individuals (just about never). For example, I told Fiona and Leo that I often feel like they are two kids fighting for my attention. I told Michael that I was impressed with how *he* had adapted to therapy and had come up with ideas for working through the trauma; I told Anne that I admired her ability to get perspective on issues, even though she feels so emotionally overwhelmed at times. I told Nick and Mirella that I, too, was stuck in getting an understanding of why they fight so much. All of these comments seemed to be taken in a way that advanced the work, which I see as the only reason to disclose countertransference reactions.

Using one's countertransference to help expand understanding and empathy, and to give partners valuable information about themselves and each other – when done consciously and deliberately, or analysed with or without the couple in retrospect – can make the treatment even more lively and current. Being a container for denied and disavowed aspects of one's patient(s) is not always a bad thing.

I want to say a few more words about the gender of the therapist, elaborating on my comments in the previous chapter. I am aware I have sometimes used the sexist term "mother" for parent, and have reported a female perspective on transference and countertransference issues. Besides the obvious reason for this, I would also like to point out that much of the recent analytically-oriented couples therapy literature has been written by women (e.g. Solomon and Siegel, 1997; Sharpe, 2000), although a significant amount of the earlier work has been done by male therapists (e.g. Dicks, 1967; Ruszczynski, 1993). Even the *New Yorker* cartoons picture female therapists for this type of work (and usually male therapists for individual therapy).

Countertransferences in male couples therapists will be different from those of female therapists; certainly, a couple must react differently to a male therapist and males must react differently to the oedipal triadic setting of couples therapy. However, the differences may not be as great as they would seem at first blush. In addition, gay or straight therapists treating gay or lesbian couples might encounter somewhat differing transferences and countertransferences. Hopefully these limitations of this book will continue to be rectified by other writers.

Chapter 7

Dénouement: working through and termination

The analytic literature on the processes of working through and termination describes the complex emotional responses that the latter, particularly, evokes in therapist and patient alike. As the reader might now expect, these processes are even more complex when they are happening with two patients at the same time.

Working through, which "permits the subject to pass from rejection [of an interpretation] or merely intellectual acceptance to a conviction based on lived experience" (Laplanche and Pontalis, 1973, p. 488), does not happen quickly, as we know from individual treatment. Despite what the movies tell us, patients rarely have an "aha" experience – exclaiming "Oh thank you, Doctor, now all is clear!" – and even more rarely do they proceed to change their behaviour if they do. Resistance to change is the most likely sequela to insight, as people are attached to their past familiar ways of relating, and even to their symptoms. In couples therapy, when a dysfunctional pattern has been identified, several interesting possibilities arise. One partner may want a change and try to move the interaction in that direction; the other, however, may see any change as threatening the relationship and therefore hang on more tightly. If the interpretation or observation originates with one of the partners, rather than with the therapist, it may be accepted more easily, because of the lack of authority-loading, or less easily, because of resentment of the other. What makes the working through more difficult with couples is that the behaviour is usually part of a long-established, collusive, way of relating; what makes it easier is that it is there in the room for all to see and experience. Also, sometimes patients in individual treatment fear the response of their partner should they begin to act differently; here, that response can be checked out, modified, and checked out again, to ensure that both partners are as much on side as possible.

Working through implies repetition, that is, new responses and behaviours have to be experienced and re-experienced many, many times, and in different ways. Sometimes one partner needs more time, or more repetitions, than the other. This is always interesting to observe; at these times, the other partner may be of help in the process. This repetitive exposure to conflicts, and the understanding and working through of them, by each individual at their own pace, is part of what accounts for the amount of time I think needs to be given to couples. When Mirella and Nick started the session after we had discussed Nick's father's diagnosis of cancer (Chapter 4) by saying "We're still fighting," it was not as surprising to me as it was to them. I knew it wasn't over yet, even though it did have a different feel to it now; but it was almost as if they expected things to change quickly and were disappointed in themselves.

Remember Chantal and Brad? Their therapy progressed, somewhat unevenly, as they worked through understanding Chantal's needs that had led to her affair, and Brad's feelings of anger, frustration, and impotence. Part of the working through process in couples, as with individuals, is the internalization of the relationship with the therapist based on new experience, as well as the development of insight through interpretation. As our work together progressed, Chantal and Brad began to feel closer to each other and closer to me. In one session, Brad commented, "We're all wearing brown today" – even though I was wearing black!

A part of their working through involved the "externalization" of the conflict around suburban living. Brad agreed to move into the city, giving up his attachment to their home, as he thought that Chantal would be happier. Discussion in the therapy revolved around compromises: i.e. could they get a house closer to the university, but with enough land so that Brad could still enjoy gardening? At this point in the therapy, a real estate agent was added to our triad – this person was talked about a great deal, as they discussed how to make their desires known to her. She tried to provide them with a solution to their city/country problem, although not exactly in a therapeutic manner. All of this time, Brad was enduring what he came to refer to as "banishment" when living in the apartment that Chantal was so reluctant to relinquish. He was anxious that Chantal might need to "break out again" even though they were in a new home, and there was some discussion about whether she needed to keep the apartment longer. Looking for the house provided them with opportunities for working through Brad's feelings about the apartment, and his lack of trust in Chantal. This led to a re-working of the affair, with material emerging again about how the former lover had been able to listen to Chantal, and to encourage her to express her feelings, something that Brad was unable to do to her satisfaction. Brad, now aware of this, tried to listen more; this was especially observable in our sessions.

Two years into treatment, *"Things are starting to feel better between them. B. really has changed, and I told him so. He is now able to listen to C.'s outpourings, which hopefully she will deliver in a manner that is considerate of him. They both said they can talk to each other more. There was some discussion of cutting back, which C. was more ready to do than B. She has gone through a lot emotionally in here – really been honest."*

Anne and Michael, the lawyers struggling with hepatitis C, began, as our work progressed, to talk about what they had hoped for when they married each other. As Michael expressed his frustration in a calmer, more reasonable, and more palatable manner, Anne noticed how she had contributed to the rage by her response of shutting down and crying, and not "getting in the ring" with him. They were now able to talk to each other in a manner that was more satisfying to both of them. I noticed, however, that once our discussions about illness and possible death were less frequent, the instant intimacy that had been generated for all three of us by this subject began to recede. As time went on, we reconnected in a more gradual way, over issues that were less emotionally charged.

They discussed the firm and how they interacted there, with Michael pointing out that Anne tended to be "officious and controlling" in meetings. She stated that this was in response to his lack of attention to detail, and his impatience with juniors who were also scared of him. All along we had understood Anne's "officiousness" as being an identification with a father who was successful in business, although cold and distant, and a disidentification with her mother, who had little education and who was treated as a "slave" by her father. Anne acknowledged that she had many of her mother's characteristics of being nurturing and reasonable; in times of stress, however, she reverted back to her identification with her father.

Michael's father, on the other hand, was unable to survive physically and mentally after losing a job when Michael was 10 years of age. He gained an enormous amount of weight, never worked again, and became diabetic and severely depressed. His mother, described as active and energetic, took over the support and maintenance of the family of four children. She, however, evidently had times of quiet desperation, when she would bang her fists against her forehead in silent, but intense, rage. We understood that the childhood experience of witnessing such inexpressible anger and frustration made a significant impression on Michael. He may have made a conscious decision to express his anger aloud so that people would hear him. In addition, his attempts to be "strong," and not like his father, were fuelling his fearsome image. Still, he did not want to cause pain to Anne or their son, or anyone at their firm. When he heard that his behaviour was affecting the juniors, he worked at being more aware in the office as well as at home.

Parallel to this, as we began to notice that Anne and Michael were "parents" everywhere but in therapy – at the firm, at home, and with their ageing parents – they both decided they needed a place to take better care of themselves and each other. They looked for and bought a beautiful home in the country, something both of them thought they would never be able to afford, as neither of their original families had managed this. This country home became not only a retreat for them and their son and other family and friends on weekends and holidays, but a place to which each of them could go separately when they needed to. This gave them some relief from the intensity of living and working together, and thereby had a general calming effect.

During this seemingly smooth working through, Michael's anger erupted at me in one session. He told me he wanted to quit therapy as he was finding the whole process too "negative." He felt that he had changed a lot, but that every time Anne got the chance to complain about him, she brought him back in the sessions to where he had been, and then we spent our time on these complaints. Anne then acknowledged that she was annoyed that I had not taken her side more, when I could see how angry Michael became. Here, finally, was some negative transference from each of them – both disappointed that I had not fixed this relationship and their individual conflicts faster and better. I was glad to hear these feelings expressed – and considered this a real step toward ending, i.e. that they were beginning to allow themselves to see me as more real, and certainly more limited, than they had imagined. I also realized that I had felt overwhelmed by the complexity of the issues: the marriage, the business, and the illness. As we talked about their frustration with the therapy, which, of course, they had talked about at home with each other, I resisted the urge to point out how different things were now from when they first came.

This couple needed to discuss their negative feelings to the fullest extent possible; also, it turned out that even though they were coming at it from different angles, they both agreed that the therapy had been a much more difficult and time-consuming process than they had ever imagined.

Leading up to termination, there were many sessions spent on the business and how to make working together less

*"It may surprise you to know that, contrary to your experience,
you're actually very happily married."*

conflicted. In some ways, the firm magnified their personality
differences: Anne as the perfect one, Michael as the angry
one. Not surprisingly, as with children in a family, these
stereotyped perceptions had been communicated to, and
accepted by, the rest of the staff. There began an interesting
process of changing these perceptions, made easier because
Anne and Michael were by then both unambivalently
involved in the process and had made it part of their job
to notice when someone was reacting to either of them in
these extreme ways. Also, they decided in the sessions how to
divide up meetings and client files, so that they became more
separate at work.

During the working through phase, as interpretations and
understanding take hold, all kinds of action plans may be
thought up and even instituted, but time and repetition are
still needed to ensure there is at least some consolidation.
One interesting sidepoint that I have noticed is that often in
this phase partners are freed up to allow the expression of
their opposite-sex characteristics. Brad's cooking lessons

were mentioned earlier. As well, when Michael was asked by Anne what he wanted for his December birthday, he revealed that he wanted to bake for a day, with his son – cookies and cakes for Christmas. Anne was surprised, and delighted, to hear this. Perhaps this is part of not having to hold on so tightly to extreme ends of a continuum, as the relationship can now bear increasing flexibility without breaking.

Termination can be a complex time for both the couple and the therapist. Here, again, I usually re-read the notes taken in the first few sessions of the treatment. This is helpful in predicting the responses to separation and ending, in noticing change that has occurred as a result of treatment, in avoiding as much as possible the repetition of earlier traumas, and in organizing the therapist's comments. The therapist's familiarity with the history helps the couple to integrate their

"First we had couples therapy, then we had you."

earlier life with the problems they have had, the work they have done, and with looking ahead to their future lives together.

Termination in couples therapy is an important phase, just as it is in work with individuals. The impetus for it can come from both partners, or from one of them. As in individual treatment, the idea of ending has to be able to be talked about without the fear of being precipitously terminated. In this modality, often it is one partner who has the courage to enquire about how the ending will happen. I then describe how they will begin to notice that they are resolving issues themselves they could not resolve earlier, that there is less fighting, that their sex life has improved, and that they actually look forward to being with their partner. They may also start to feel that the therapy is becoming a "nuisance" and inconvenient, and that there is not much to talk about except to report successes; another criterion I sometimes offer in helping them to decide is to consider whether they would initiate therapy right now, if they were not already here. In most situations, when both partners are ready to end, we set a date together, usually a few months in advance, and work toward that date.

In psychoanalysis and psychoanalytic psychotherapy, criteria for ending include the resolution of the transference, a more equitable relationship with the therapist, the resolution of early conflicts, particularly with parents and siblings, and as Freud said, an increased capacity to love and to work.

In couples therapy, there is some of this and more. The therapist does become more realistically viewed, but that is usually not so difficult as, first, the therapist is more active in this type of work and, second, the focus is on the two individuals. The criterion that is most important with couples is, to state it broadly, "symptom" improvement: that is, the easing of, or resolution of, the presenting problems; a more comprehensive understanding by both partners as to why and how conflicts arose in the relationship; a more realistic perception of *each other*, with, as much as possible, the resolution of maladaptive partner-to-partner transferences; a greater tolerance for flaws and times of weakness in the other; a better way of communicating to each other; a way of providing a holding environment for the other; ways of meeting a partner's selfobject needs, when appropriate; and a way of empathizing with one's partner so that each individual can, at least at times, feel deeply understood by the other.

"My wife understands me."

Yet another very tall order. However, these are guidelines to which the couples therapist can refer mentally as the therapy evolves and as this phase unfolds. The ideal termination – when everyone feels content that the therapeutic work is "finished," and that the ending is nothing more than a smooth outgrowth of the therapy – is probably about as rare with couples as it is in individual treatment.

As sometimes happens during the termination phase of individual therapy, couples may experience a revival of their earlier symptoms – for example, problems with sexual expression, old arguments that haven't been fought for a while, or unresolved partner-to-partner transferences. These flare-ups have to be taken at face value, and further working through may be required. Also, interpretations regarding how each individual sees termination – for example, anxiety or feelings of guilt about achieving independence as an adult couple – can be very productive. Couples, like individuals, will reminisce during the ending phase about their thinking when they first came, their expectations of the therapy, and goals that have been met and not met.

As has been mentioned earlier, it often happens that as a couple move into the termination phase, they may spend more time on extra-couple issues, by mutual agreement. Even though subjects such as one partner's work, difficulties with children, or care of parents can be woven into the middle phase of therapy, they seem more prominent in this phase. It is as if before taking their leave, they want to make use of this safe environment to clear up whatever else they can in their lives. This is often a very productive use of time, as both people are present, and the therapy often moves along fairly quickly. Sometimes one partner's problem has been affecting both people and neither have ever had the chance to talk about it or to hear about it in a focussed way.

For example, near the end of our work together, Anne raised the issue that she was frightened to drive (that was news to me), and related it to being hit by a car at age 5. She remembered the clothes she was wearing at the time, but had no affective memory of the incident. She said that as an adult, she always takes taxis, but would like to be able to drive. We spent some time on this, and discovered that Michael was not only not bothered by her phobia but, in fact, found it quite handy as he got the car all the time. This led to a productive interchange about his contribution to the perpetuation of her fear, which she had not known about – and to further exploration of the dynamic of dependence–independence in their relationship. I can't claim that we cured the phobia, but we did give it a different slant. Anne said she was at least able to consider driving lessons, although she did not feel ready to make the move.

Because there are two individuals, there can sometimes be a discrepancy in desires and motivations for ending. It may happen that one partner wants to, or even is ready to, terminate earlier than the other. In this case, it is always helpful to examine the individual motives for termination. In the case of Diane and Tom (Diane had acted as a surrogate mother for her sister), although Tom was trying to cooperate throughout the treatment, one got the sense that he would rather be on the squash court. About six months into it, when the first crises had been resolved, Diane suggested termination, saying she felt much better about Tom, that he was now easier to live with, and that she thought they could move ahead on their own. My first thought was that Tom had instructed her to say this; it was denied by both. Then I suggested that she was worried about delving more deeply into their problems for fear the relationship might suffer a fatal blow. Both paused on this one; Diane said she didn't think so, but that she just felt ready to end. Tom was certainly ready to stop. So, with some misgivings, I agreed, of course instructing them to call should any difficulties arise. Four sessions later, we shook hands and said goodbye. In the above situation, I persuaded them to stay another month, as I hoped for a better understanding for all of us of what was transpiring. This was not to happen at that time.

Six weeks later I got a call from Diane requesting, nay, begging, to come for individual therapy. She felt she had finally found someone with whom she could talk, and wanted to set up weekly sessions with me – the motive behind the rush to end. This is difficult, and a lot of therapists would not agree with me on this point. I said I was really sorry, because I liked her and felt I could work with her, but I wanted to remain a resource for them as a couple. If we began individual sessions, they would lose this should they need it again. I gave her the name of a colleague I thought she would like, but she did not contact this colleague, as far as I knew.

As I write, I still feel unsure about this – it probably reflected too rigid a boundary on my part.

About five months before Anne and Michael ended, Michael broached the subject of termination, asking how they would know when to leave. My response was that I saw them as having one foot on solid ground and that they were almost ready to put the other foot over. I asked them to talk more about ending. Anne felt they needed more time, and wanted reassurance that they would be the ones to decide. Once the topic has been raised, I encourage couples to make it one of the themes of the ongoing therapy.

Countertransference feelings and fantasies are often painfully evoked during a couple's termination phase. How much of a selfobject has this couple been for the therapist? How much of a holding environment has been provided in *both* directions? What did the couple represent for the therapist, and what does saying goodbye to them mean? Oedipal issues, present throughout most of the work, now rise up in a significant way. Did the therapist get the chance to fix his or her parents? Or to be parented by them? Does the therapist feel reluctant to end because he or she is disappointed in how far the treatment went? Or is the therapist relieved to see these warring people leave and to restore quiet and calm in the office? Unresolved separation issues in the therapist also come to the surface, as they do in the termination of any analytically oriented work. Is the therapist able to let the couple go? The therapist's needs are, consciously or unconsciously, a part of the couple's decision to terminate. We can hold the couple back, lingering over the positive, warm feelings we have established together as a threesome; or we can hurry them along, evacuating the negative or envious emotions they stir up.

When Chantal and Brad began to talk about ending, I thought, "*I will really miss them.*" The beginning of their ending phase was heralded by my asking the question – which seemed to me to be in the air, but not being addressed: does Chantal still need space, and what is the function of the downtown apartment now? I also articulated for them that

Brad did not want to move into the city, and that he was making a very difficult choice by doing so, hoping for a better relationship. Chantal, for her part, was still worried about being "smothered" when they found a house and moved in together. We talked about this for several sessions; our brilliant compromise was starting to sound like a problem for both of them. This needed more discussion. After some time, they agreed to try the compromise and asked to cut back their frequency to once a month.

Three months later: *"Termination – almost. Both reporting things are going well. C. still hanging onto the apartment which B. hates. Taking the reins again, since they are so reluctant to, I asked directly how vulnerable C. feels to another affair. She was very reassuring about this. B. got uncomfortable, but I said I just wanted to check things out – knowing that he must, too. They had set a date together to end, but told me B. had 'chickened out.'"*

As we tried to understand the meaning of the ending for each of them, I also tried to understand the meaning of it for me. That I would miss them has already been said. But I also was worried about letting them go before all the loose ends had been tied up (e.g. the apartment, the new house, Brad feeling even more trusting of Chantal). By forcing myself to listen to them, however, I was able to hear that they wanted to solve some of these issues on their own. Again, this may be a difference with couples therapy: they have each other with whom to continue the work and are keen to try out what they have learned; they don't feel as alone as an individual does at termination. We set a date.

They were both excited to come to their last session. Although Brad was still somewhat wary about ending, he said he really wanted to try it. "Could you phone us in a couple of months to see how we're doing?" he asked me. I said they were welcome to call me at any time. "We'll probably have other issues, maybe not about each other, but about our parents," he said. It was clear to me that he had not only formed a strong attachment to me, but also had "gotten it" – in terms of what therapy is about. Probably because the ending was hard for all three of us, we decided to have a check-in appointment three months later. Chantal was the one who set it up. This is not typical for me, but on the other hand, I don't refuse it if both partners want to meet once more (and naturally I have the desire to see how they are doing). An expression I sometimes use at termination time, with individuals and with couples, is that if they ever feel the need to do "post-graduate work," they can always come back. This gives them the sense of accomplishment that comes from having graduated, and also leaves the door ajar in a non-pejorative way in case further contact is needed.

In our last few months of work together, Anne and Michael began cutting back their frequency in what seemed like a "reasonable" way, in that their work was extremely busy and time seemed short for them. What was happening, in fact, was that they were no longer sacrificing everything at the office for their therapy sessions; in other words, therapy was less important, less desperate. They also took more holidays together for longer periods of time. As they moved toward thoughts of ending, both began spontaneously to talk about when they first came, what problems were on their minds, and how they had felt about each other. Anne also took the opportunity to say she still wasn't sure the issue of handling the hepatitis C was completely dealt with. This made Michael angry at first; then, he was able to really see how much he disliked talking about it. They decided on a method for broaching the subject: Anne would say: "I feel the need to say something about it now, is this a good time?" Both agreed to this. I noticed that they talked more and more to each other in the sessions, and hardly needed or wanted much from me.

The idea of ending seemed to be in the minds of both partners when they noticed that they did well during their periods of absence from the therapy – either their holidays or mine. When this happened, and it was actually articulated, Anne brought in worries about their son's school where there were classroom size problems, stating they needed to make a decision now as to whether he should switch schools. They talked about this in a seemingly productive way, and in the next session she talked about needing to persuade her parents to sell their home as it was too big for them. Again Michael readily joined in – maybe relieved that the complaints had nothing to do with him. By this time I was thinking: either Anne is not ready to end, or she feels she'll never have Michael's attention again in this way, and needs to discuss these issues with him – or both. I mentioned these observations to them.

Anne agreed on both counts. We had the chance to discuss her fears about ending – that Michael would revert to his angry self, that she would feel terribly alone, and that they wouldn't be able to talk outside the sessions the way they could when we were together. I also mentioned that her anxiety about Michael possibly becoming ill again might be getting displaced onto the subject of his anger – which had, for the most part, come under control. We talked again about Michael's medical situation and prognosis. Michael then said reassuringly to Anne: "You've seen how I don't get as angry anymore. And we can talk about so many things, even my illness – I'll try to keep this up as much as I can, because I want it, too. It's been so much better for me over the last while. I really feel happy to be married to you." We all beamed.

The process of termination was now rolling: they made an official cutback in frequency, first to every second week, then to once per month. During this time, Anne discovered a lump in her left breast. I was tempted to try an interpretation, linking the lump to her anxiety about our termination, hoping she'd say: "You're right!" and then the lump would disappear – but even my grandiosity could not be stretched that far. The termination process was now derailed; I tried to maintain the holding environment in which they had conquered so many fears. We waited together for the results of various tests. When the results of the biopsy came back resoundingly negative, we breathed a collective sigh of relief. Michael had been very supportive during this period, which had helped Anne to feel she could depend on him again, a feeling she had not had for many years.

In our last session, they brought in photographs of their families – their parents, their son, and their brother and sisters. I was interested to "meet" these people we had talked so much about, and to hear further discussion of them. Was I now a part of that family? Probably – in the strange way we therapists tend to be – present in our patients' psychic families, if not in their "real" ones.

A common response of therapists to ending, according to Firestein (1978), is anxiety about the results of the work – whether it has been sufficiently thoroughgoing. With Anne and Michael, I had the added countertransference burden of trying to evaluate the experience related to the illness and dying that I had so recently endured with my own analyst. I was aware of a desire to continue to help them, when they no longer needed my help (at least not at that time). As Shane and Shane (1984) have indicated, the quality and resolution of the separation and mourning process by the therapist at termination time depend on their previous experience with separation from parents, *and* in their own therapy; their ability to master their own therapeutic ambition; and their finely-tuned self-analysing functions. Self-analysis in this situation (which I did in the form of journaling) was extremely useful.

It seems to me that what is mourned and relinquished for the couple in ending this work is not so much the therapist, as the holding environment that was created by all three participants – which allowed them to talk, confidentially, to another person and to each other about private and difficult matters. This threesome will never be the same again. The hope, of course, is that the feeling and experience have been internalized sufficiently and can be carried on without the therapist; but the room, the time, the space will necessarily be different. If the therapist has allowed for the door to always be open for couples who may want to return, they will usually find that they do not come back, and that if they do, the issues are new and very different. This allows for a great deal of optimism about the couple's ability to help each other to internalize and remember what they have worked so hard to learn about each other.

What we call the beginning is often the end
And to make an end is to make a beginning.
The end is where we start from.
(T.S. Eliot, "Little Gidding")

Bibliography

Altman, L.L. (1977). Some vicissitudes of love. *Journal of the American Psychoanalytic Association, 25*, 35–52.

Aron, L. (1996). *A meeting of minds: mutuality in psychoanalysis.* Hillsdale, NJ: The Analytic Press.

Atwood, G. and Stolorow, R. (1984). *Structures of subjectivity.* Hillsdale, NJ: The Analytic Press.

Bacal, H.A. and Newman, K.M. (1990). *Theories of object relations: bridges to self psychology.* New York: Columbia University Press.

Bak, R.C. (1973). Being in love and object loss. *International Journal of Psycho-Analysis, 54*, 1–8.

Bank, S.P. and Kahn, M.D. (1982). *The sibling bond.* New York: Basic Books, Inc.

Bergmann, M.S. (1980). On the intrapsychic function of falling in love. *Psychoanalytic Quarterly, 49*, 56–77.

—— (1982). Platonic love, transference love and love in real life. *Journal of the American Psychoanalytic Association, 30*, 87–111.

Berkowitz, D.A. (1999). Reversing the negative cycle: interpreting the mutual influence of adaptive, self-protective measures in the couple. *Psychoanalytic Quarterly, 68*, 559–583.

Blum, H.P. (1986). Countertransference and the theory of technique. *Journal of the American Psychoanalytic Association, 34*, 309–328.

Brown, L.J. (2002). The early oedipal situation: developmental, theoretical, and clinical implications. *The Psychoanalytic Quarterly, LXXI*, 273–300.

Cleavely, E. (1993). Relationships: interaction, defences, and transformation. In *Psychotherapy with couples*, ed. S. Ruszczynski. London: Karnac Books.

Cohen, L. (1993). *Stranger music: selected poems and songs.* Toronto: McClelland & Stewart Inc.

Cohen, P. (1999). Psychoanalytically informed short-term couple therapy. In *Short-term couple therapy*, ed. J.M. Donovan. New York: Guilford Press.

Colarusso, C.A. (1990). The third individuation – the effect of biological parenthood on separation-individuation processes in adulthood. *Psychoanalytic Study of the Child*, *45*, 179–194.

—— (2000). Separation-individuation phenomena in adulthood: general concepts and the fifth individuation. *Journal of the American Psychoanalytic Association*, *48*, 1468–1489.

Colman, W. (1993). Marriage as a psychological container. In *Psychotherapy with couples*, ed. S. Ruszczynski. London: Karnac Books.

Dicks, H.V. (1967). *Marital tensions: clinical studies towards a psychological theory of interaction.* London: Karnac Books.

Eissler, K.R. (1955). *The psychiatrist and the dying patient.* New York: International Universities Press.

Epstein, L. and Feiner, A.H. (1993). *Countertransference: the therapist's contribution to the therapeutic situation.* Northvale, NJ: Jason Aronson Inc.

Finkelstein, L. (1988). Psychoanalysis, marital therapy, and object-relations theory. *Journal of the American Psychoanalytic Association*, *36*, 905–931.

Firestein, S.K. (1978). *Termination in psychoanalysis.* New York: International Universities Press.

Frank, J.A. (1997). Oedipal countertransference in marital therapy. In *Countertransference in couples therapy*, ed. M.F. Solomon and J.P. Siegel. New York: W.W. Norton & Company.

Frayn, D.H. (2005). *Understanding your dreams: a guide to self-awareness.* Toronto: Ash Productions.

Freud, S. (1905). *Three essays on the theory of sexuality.* Standard Edition, VII, pp. 135–243.

—— (1910). *A special type of object choice made by men (Contributions to the psychology of love I).* Standard Edition, XI, pp. 165–175.

—— (1912). *On the universal tendency to debasement in the sphere of love (Contributions to the psychology of love II).* Standard Edition, XI, pp. 179–190.

—— (1914). *On narcissism: an introduction.* Standard Edition, XIV, pp. 73–102.

—— (1915a). *Observations on transference-love*. Standard Edition, XII, pp. 158–171.

—— (1915b). *Instincts and their vicissitudes*. Standard Edition, XIV, pp. 117–140.

Galatzer-Levy, R.M. (2004). The death of the analyst. *Journal of the American Psychoanalytic Association, 52(4)*, 999–1024.

Garza-Guerrero, C. (2000). Idealization and mourning in love relationships: normal and pathological spectra. *The Psychoanalytic Quarterly, 69*, 121–150.

Gay, P. (1988). *Freud: a life for our time*. New York: W.W. Norton & Company.

Gill, M.M. (1955). *Analysis of transference* (Psychological Issues Monograph No. 53). New York: International Universities Press.

Ginot, E. (2001). The holding environment and intersubjectivity. *The Psychoanalytic Quarterly, 70(2)*, 417–446.

Greenberg, J.R. and Mitchell, S.A. (1983). *Object relations in psychoanalytic theory*. Cambridge, MA: Harvard University Press.

Greenson, R.R. (1967). *The technique and practice of psychoanalysis*. Madison, CT: International Universities Press.

Gurman, A.S. and Jacobson, N.S., eds (2002). *Clinical handbook of couple therapy*. New York: Guilford Press.

Guttman, H.A. (1982). Transference and countertransference in conjoint couple therapy: therapeutic and theoretical implications. *Canadian Journal of Psychiatry, 27*, 92–97.

Harway, M., ed. (2005). *Handbook of couples therapy*. New York: John Wiley & Sons, Inc.

Jacobs, T.J. (1986). On countertransference enactments. *Journal of the American Psychoanalytic Society, 34*, 289–307.

—— (1991). *The use of self: countertransference and communication in the analytic situation*. Madison, CT: International Universities Press.

Kalb, M.B. (2002). Does sex matter? The confluence of gender and transference in analytic space. *Psychoanalytic Psychology, 19*, 118–143.

Kernberg, O.F. (1974). Barriers to falling and remaining in love. *Journal of the American Psychoanalytic Association, 22*, 486–511.

—— (1991). Aggression and love in the relationship of the couple. *Journal of the American Psychoanalytic Association, 39*, 45–70.

—— (1995). *Love relations: normality and pathology*. New Haven: Yale University Press.

Kipnis, L. (2003). *Against love: a polemic*. New York: Pantheon Books.

Kluger, J. (2006). The new science of siblings. *Time*, *168*, 31–39.

Kohut, H. (1971). *The analysis of the self*. New York: International Universities Press.

—— (1977). *The restoration of the self*. New York: International Universities Press.

—— (1984). *How does analysis cure?* Chicago: University of Chicago Press.

Kulosh, N. and Mayman, M. (1993). Gender-linked determinants of transference and countertransference in psychoanalytic psychotherapy. *Psychoanalytic Inquiry*, *13*, 286–305.

Laplanche, J. and Pontalis, J.B. (1973). *The language of psychoanalysis*. London: W.W. Norton & Company.

Lawrence, D.H. (2002). *Women in love*. New York: The Modern Library.

Lennon, C. (2005). *John*. New York: Crown Publishers.

Lyons, A. (1993). Husbands and wives: the mysterious choice. In *Psychotherapy with couples*. ed. S. Ruszczynski. London: Karnac Books.

McLaughlin, J. (1991). Clinical and theoretical aspects of enactment. *Journal of the American Psychoanalytic Association*, *39*, 595–614.

Mahler, M. (1963). Thoughts about development and individuation. *The Psychoanalytic Study of the Child*, *18*, 307–324.

—— (1974). Symbiosis and individuation: the psychological birth of the human infant. In *The Selected Papers of Margaret S. Mahler*, vol. 2. New York: Jason Aronson.

Mead, R. (2003). Love's labours. *The New Yorker*, 11 August.

Miller, M.V. (1995). *Intimate terrorism: the deterioration of erotic life*. New York: W.W. Norton & Company.

Mitchell, S.A. (2002). *Can love last? The fate of romance over time*. New York: W.W. Norton & Company.

Mitchell, S.A. and Black, M.J. (1995). *Freud and beyond*. New York: Basic Books.

Novick, J. (1982). Termination: themes and issues. *Psychoanalytic Inquiry*, *2(3)*, 329–365.

Ogden, T. (1982). *Projective identification and psychotherapeutic technique*. New York: Jason Aronson.

—— (1994). The analytic third: working with intersubjective clinical facts. *International Journal of Psychoanalysis*, 75, 3–19.

Racker, H. (1968). *Transference and countertransference.* New York: International Universities Press.

Rangell, L. (1982). Some thoughts on termination. *Psychoanalytic Inquiry*, 2(3), 367–392.

Renik, O. (1993). Analytic interaction: conceptualizing technique in light of the analyst's irreducible subjectivity. *The Psychoanalytic Quarterly*, 62, 553–571.

Ross, J.M. (1991). A psychoanalytic essay on romantic, erotic love. *Journal of the American Psychoanalytic Association*, 39S, 439–475.

Rothstein, A. (1992). Observations on the utility of couples therapy conducted by a psychoanalyst – transference and countertransference in resistance to analysis. *The Psychoanalytic Quarterly*, 61, 519–541.

Ruszczynski, S., ed. (1993). *Psychotherapy with couples: theory and practice at the Tavistock Institute of Marital Studies.* London: Karnac Books.

Sager, C.J. (1994). *Marriage contracts and couple therapy: hidden forces in intimate relationships.* Northvale, NJ: Jason Aronson.

Sandler, J. (1976). Countertransference and role-responsiveness. *International Review of Psychoanalysis*, 3, 43–47.

Sandler, J., Dare, C., and Holder, A. (1973). *The patient and the analyst: the basis of the psychoanalytic process.* Madison, CT: International Universities Press.

Scharff, D.D. and Scharff, J. (1991). *Object relations couple therapy.* Northvale, NJ: Jason Aronson.

Searles, H.F. (1979). *Countertransference and related subjects.* New York: International Universities Press.

Shane, M. and Shane, E. (1984). The end phase of analysis: indicators, functions, and tasks of termination. *Journal of the American Psychoanalytic Association*, 32, 739–772.

Sharpe, S.A. (2000). *The ways we love: a developmental approach to treating couples.* New York: Guilford Press.

Sharpe, S.A. and Rosenblatt, A.D. (1994). Oedipal sibling triangles. *Journal of the American Psychoanalytic Association*, 42(2), 491–523.

Sharpe, S.S. (1997). Countertransference and diagnosis in couples therapy. In *Countertransference in couples therapy*, ed. M.F. Solomon and J.P. Siegel. New York: W.W. Norton & Company.

Solomon, M.F. (1994). *Lean on me: the power of positive dependency in intimate relationships.* New York: Simon & Schuster.

Solomon, M.F. and Siegel, J.P., eds (1997). *Countertransference in couples therapy.* New York: W.W. Norton & Company.

Spurling, L. (2003). On psychoanalytic figures as transference objects. *International Journal of Psychoanalysis, 8,* 31–43.

Stoller, R.J. (1991). Hooray for love. *Journal of the American Psychoanalytic Association, 39S,* 413–435.

Turkel, A.R. (1992). The gender of the analyst. *International Forum of Psychoanalysis, 1,* 11–19.

Usher, S.F. (1993). *Introduction to psychoanalytic psychotherapy technique.* Madison, CT: International Universities Press.

Wallerstein, J.S. and Blakeslee, S. (1995). *The good marriage: how and why love lasts.* New York: Warner Books.

West, J.J. and Schain-West, J. (1997). Envy in the countertransference. In *Countertransference in couples therapy,* ed. M.F. Solomon and J.P. Siegel. New York: W.W. Norton & Company.

Winnicott, D. (1965). *The maturational process and the facilitating environment.* London: Hogarth Press.

Index

abandonment 12, 18, 33, 79, 113–14, 118
abortion 43, 65
acting out 26
ADHD *see* attention deficit hyperactivity disorder
adolescence 61
affairs 35, 57, 77, 88–9, 90, 137
aggression 5, 54–5, 59–60, 65
Altman, L.L. 61–2, 67
ambivalence 9, 54, 61, 64, 75
anger 66, 78, 90, 92, 94, 149; critical incidents 43, 44; in loving relationships 61; negative transference 139; parental 138; presentation of problems 31, 32, 33; stored up 41; *see also* rage
anxiety 6, 12
attachment 4, 21, 47
attention deficit hyperactivity disorder (ADHD) 94, 95
attunement 39, 71, 97
Atwood, G. 28
autonomy 3
avoidance 121

Bak, R.C. 53
Berkowitz, D.A. 70
Bion, Wilfred 22, 24
bipolar disorder 50
blame 32–3, 81

blended families 35–6
borderline personality disorder 50
boundary setting 132
bullying 129–31

children 42, 77, 78, 91; blended families 35–6; inclusion in therapy session 106; mother/child dyad 13, 17–18, 24, 53; object relations 20; parents' separation 99–100; therapist as child 120–1
classical theory viii, 2, 3–11, 80
Cleavely, E. 3
co-therapist concept 81, 82, 109
cognitive-behavioural theory 1
Cohen, Leonard 54
Cohen, P. 2, 4
Colarusso, C.A. 13
collusion 47, 85
Colman, W. 22, 103
communication 84, 91, 137, 143; countertransference 132; diffusion of ambivalence 75; of needs and motivations 71; about sex 46
competition 85, 107
conflict resolution 142–3
conjoint therapy 29
containment 22, 24, 39, 92
contempt 121
contract theory 1–2

countertransference ix, 5, 15, 79, 101, 116–34; co-construction of 28; erotic fantasy 111; holding environment 28; Kleinian approach 18; 'negative' 127–31; 'positive' 122–7; termination of therapy 146, 150
countertransference love 63
crises 97–8, 102
critical incidents 40–5, 47, 123
cultural issues 36

de-idealization 60, 61–2, 63–4
death 123, 124, 125, 126, 127, 137
defence ix, 5, 32–3
defences 3, 6, 60, 62, 64, 110
defensiveness 39, 76
denial 110
dependence 21, 22, 47
depression 96, 97, 98
desire 47, 50, 68, 89
devaluation 60, 62, 63–4, 121
Dicks, H.V. 21, 75
disappointment 60, 62, 64, 67
divorce 59, 67, 68, 70
domestic violence 128–9
dreams 80, 84–5, 86–7, 124–5
drives viii, 4

ego 4, 20
ego-ideal 51
Eliot, T.S. 151
empathy 26, 71, 93, 133, 143
enactment 109, 117
envy 18, 51, 112, 119, 121–2
erotic feelings 59
erotic transference 110–11
expectations ix, x, 62, 102, 114, 119
extra-marital affairs 35, 57, 77, 88–9, 90, 137

Fairbairn, W.R.D. 17, 20–1, 22, 52, 63

family issues 34–5; blended families 35–6; history-taking 37–9; see also parents; siblings
fantasies 4, 104, 105, 111, 119
father 65, 138; see also parents
fear 65
Finkelstein, L. 17
Firestein, S.K. 150
forgiveness 71
formulation 47–8
Frank, J.A. 112, 118, 120–1
free association 80, 84, 86–7
Freud, Sigmund 4–5, 51; countertransference 116–17; debasement 57; hate 54; intrapsychic theory 17; love 68, 142; object choice 55; passionate letters to Martha 55; transference 101

Gay, P. 116–17
gay therapists 134
gender of therapist 104–5, 106, 134
Ginot, E. 27–8
'gold-digger' case 127–8
'good-enough' mother 24
grandiosity 30, 119, 132
Greenson, R.R. 102
guilt 6, 9, 100, 124; blended families 36; motivation for therapy 34; separation 13; termination of therapy 144
Guttman, H.A. 103

hate 18, 67; co-existence with love 54, 61; containment by therapist 76; siblings 59
healing 26–7
history-taking 5, 26, 37–40, 67, 72
holding 39, 47
holding environment 46, 96, 143; intersubjectivity 27–8; termination phase 146, 149, 150; Winnicott 24

homosexuality x, 55; *see also* gay
    therapists
humour xii, 93

idealization 83, 89, 114–15; envy
    121; internal parents 112; love
    51–2, 60, 62, 63, 64; oedipal
    conflict 131; selfobject functions
    26; siblings 59; transferences to
    the therapist 104; whole couple
    transference 110
in-laws 34
incest 55, 57, 58
individual agendas 33–4, 36, 100
individual therapy 29, 73, 77, 85–6,
    87–8; client's request for 145–6;
    dreams 84, 85; negative aspects of
    30; silences 82; termination phase
    142, 143–4; transference 112;
    working through 136
individuation 11, 12, 13, 21, 112,
    113; *see also* separation
internal objects 17
interpretation 6, 28, 41, 80–1;
    dreams 85, 87; termination of
    therapy 144; transference 103;
    working through 135, 136, 140
intersubjectivity 27–8, 114
intimacy 3, 6, 8, 22, 69, 137–8;
    conflicts around 33; fear of 11, 81;
    need for 47; oppositional couples
    113; sex as defence against 122;
    symbiotic couples 113

jokes xii, 110

Kalb, M.B. 105
Kipnis, L. 50
Klein, Melanie 18
Kleinian approach 18–19, 20
Kluger, J. 37
Kohut, Heinz 25–6, 51, 71, 114
Kulosh, N. 104

Laplanche, J. 51, 135
latency 61
Lawrence, D.H. 68
learning disability 94–5
Lennon, John 56–7
lesbian therapists 134
libido 17, 20
long-term treatment xi, 73
love 18, 49–71; criteria for ending
    therapy 142; de-idealization 60,
    61–2, 63–4; idealization 51–2, 59,
    60, 62, 63, 64; mature 69–70;
    merging 51, 52–3; object choice
    55–60; sex and passion 47, 53–5;
    siblings 59; staying in love 66–71
Lyons, A. 5–6, 67

Mahler, Margaret 8, 11–12, 13, 17,
    21, 22
marriage x, 61–2, 66–7
masturbation 57
mature love 69–70
Mayman, M. 104
McLaughlin, J. 109, 132
mental representations 4
merging 51, 52–3, 131
middle phase of treatment 79–100
Miller, M.V. 69
Milton, John 68
mirroring 26, 56, 62, 114–15
Mitchell, S.A. 60, 64, 66, 69
money issues 7, 32
mother 6, 7, 8–9, 138; containment
    22; 'good-enough' 24; mother/
    child dyad 13, 17–18, 24, 53;
    separation from 14–17; *see also*
    parents

narcissism 10, 118; idealization 51;
    object choice 4–5; partner-to-
    partner transferences 115;
    vulnerability 76, 83
nymphomania 50

object choice 4–5, 18–19, 37, 55–60
object relations viii, 2, 11–25; countertransference 133; love 52; partners' role-taking 83; reliving of conflicts 102
observing ego 4
obsessive compulsive disorder 50
oedipal conflict 5, 6, 131; countertransference 118; termination phase 146; transference 103, 112
oedipal sibling triangles 58–9
Oko, Yoko 56, 57
'one-person' theory viii, 2; see also classical theory
opening phase of treatment 73–9
oppositional couples 113
overdetermination 4

parents 5, 8–9, 63, 138–9; countertransference 120; death of 44; experience of parents' love and marriage 67; internal psychic model 112; parental transference 105–6; selfobject functions 26; separation from 12, 13, 14, 15; see also father; mother
partner choice 4–5, 18–19, 37, 55–60
passion 50, 53–5, 67, 69
past relationships 38
Pontalis, J.B. 51, 135
pornography 55, 57
'post-graduate work' 148
pregnancy 43, 65–6
primary gain 4
projection 5, 19, 20, 60, 67–8
projective identification ix, 18–19, 22, 83, 118, 132–3
psychoanalysis viii–ix, 2; classical theory viii, 2, 3–11, 80; criteria for ending therapy 142; interpretation 80;

intersubjectivity 27–8, 114; love 50; relational theory viii, 28, 117; self psychology 25–7; transference 101–2; see also Freud; object relations
psychopathology 20, 27, 114
psychosexual development 4

rage 14, 22–3, 64, 98, 137; narcissistic 26; parental 65, 138; Swept Away 54–5; therapists' focus on 118; see also anger
regression 20–1, 106, 119
relational theory viii, 28, 117
relationship dynamics 82–3, 84, 108
religious issues 36
Renik, Owen 28, 102
reparation 67
repetition compulsion 4, 20
report cards 80, 107, 109
resistance ix, 5, 108, 130, 135
role-responsiveness 83, 133
romance 50–1
Rosenblatt, A.D. 58–9
Ross, J.M. 55
Ruszczynski, S. 18, 19, 25

Sager, C.J. ix–x
same-sex rivalry 118
Sandler, J. 83, 133
Schain-West, J. 121, 122
secondary gain 4
self ix, 51, 53
self-analysis 150
self psychology 25–7
selfobject 25–6, 52, 56, 114–15, 143
separation 8, 11–13, 14, 15–17, 20, 21–2; as an 'attitude' 81, 82; oppositional couples 113; partner-to-partner transferences 112; symbiotic couples 113; termination of therapy 141, 146, 150; therapy directed towards 98–100

sex 31, 45–7, 53–5, 88, 111, 122
sexual abuse 87, 88, 89
sexuality 98, 99
Shakespeare, William 50
Shane, E. 150
Shane, M. 150
Sharpe, S.A. 58–9, 62, 113, 119, 131
siblings: history-taking 37–8; influence on partner choice 37, 58–9; transference 106–7, 112
Siegel, J.P. 118
silences 82
splitting 62–3, 110
stages of treatment: formulation 47–8; history-taking 37–40; middle phase 79–100; opening phase 73–9; presentation of problems 30–7; termination 141–50
Stoller, R.J. 49, 50–1, 55
Stolorow, R. 27, 28
subjectivity 27, 28, 102, 117
surrogate pregnancy 42–3
Swept Away (film) 54–5
symbiotic couples 113
systems theory 1

tender affection 68, 69
terminal illness 123–7
termination of therapy 73, 100, 135, 141–50
therapeutic relationship 4, 84, 85, 142
therapists 1, 25, 73; containment of hatred and hopelessness 76; countertransference 116–34; couple assessment of 79; dream interpretation 87; emotional involvement 27–8; gender of 104–5, 106, 134; role-

responsiveness 83; separation issues 12–13; termination of therapy 146, 150; transference 102, 103, 104–12; working through 136
'third' 6, 9, 10
'third area' 25
'third individuation' 13
tolerance 71, 143
transference ix, 5, 79, 101–15; co-construction of 28; criteria for ending therapy 142; different reactions between partners 108–9; dream interpretation 87; early object relations 83; erotic 110–11; family histories 38–9; gender of therapist 104–5, 106; holding environment 28; idealizing 74; Kleinian approach 18; negative 139; parental 105–6; partner-to-partner 103, 112–15, 142–3, 144; selfobject 26; sibling 37, 106–7, 112; whole couple 109–10, 111
transference love 63
Turkel, A.R. 104
twinship 26, 114–15
two-person therapy 102

the unconscious 2, 80

voyeurism 118, 120
vulnerability 76, 83

Wertmuller, Lina 54
West, J.J. 121, 122
whole couple transference 109–10, 111
Winnicott, D.W. 23–4, 25, 51
work 10, 138, 139–40
working through 135–41